Abo
autl

Penelope Leach
world's leading
of many books
(Dorling Kinder
(Dorling Kinder
Visiting Profess
and Hon. Snr. R
Children, Famil
London, and at
co-directed the
familieschildrer
research into th
childcare on ch

Penelope has al
children and pa
National Child
of the National
and a founding
of Children (nov
for Infant Ment
concerns for children to the attention of politicians and policy
makers that she became a founding Director of the Mindful
Policy Group.

Penelope is mother of two and grandmother of six, and lives in
East Sussex.

This book is dedicated to the three-year-old girl who told me
"Go on, go on. Write. Write it down what I'm telling you."

Family
Breakdown

Family Breakdown

Helping children hang on to both their parents

Penelope Leach

unbound

This edition first published in 2014

Unbound
4–7 Manchester Street, Marylebone, London, W1U 2AE
www.unbound.co.uk

Typeset by GreenGate Publishing Services, Tonbridge, Kent
Cover design by Mecob

A CIP record for this book is available from the British Library

ISBN 978-1-78352-049-7
ISBN 978-1-78352-050-3 (ebook)

Printed in England by Arnold Moon Ltd

Contents

Acknowledgements

I have been amassing material about parental separation for a long time, and hundreds of people have helped me by sharing their experiences. I owe special thanks to the many children and parents who talked to me and some of whom, thoroughly anonymied, are quoted in the book.

A book of this kind relies on so many sources of research and opinion that only a small selection could appear in the research, fact and quote boxes and the reference list at the back. I gratefully acknowledge my debt to all the rest.

Family Breakdown: Helping children hang on to both their parents is intended to make things better for children whose parents separate or divorce, and to this end friends and colleagues have given most generously of their time and expertise. In particular I should like to thank Jane McDonagh of Simons, Muirhead & Bowen for her unfailing support; Sir Paul Coleridge for his foreword; my fellow directors of the Mindful Policy Group for all their support; Jon Akass whose film helped bring the issue to the attention of family lawyers; Alexander Gregory whose video put the book on social media and Sarah Kemp who always steered me in the right direction at the right moment.

Finally, I am immeasurably grateful to my publisher, Unbound and its team, especially to Dan Kieran for his generosity and to Luke Neima for editing that was unfailingly both patient and creative.

Foreword
By Sir Paul Coleridge

I have been involved in the awful business of family breakdown
for my entire professional life, so far some 42 years. And it is,
make no mistake, an awful business. For almost the entirety of
that time I have also been married, and to the same woman.
Sometimes, half jokingly, at the beginning or end of a talk on
some family or family law-related topic, I say that this means
I have a total of 80 years' experience. By that I mean I have
experienced both the wonder and deep consolation of family
life and the pain of family breakdown in roughly equal amounts.
So in general I regard myself as better qualified than many to
express an opinion on both. In particular I think it entitles me to
consider the value of this book.

In the United Kingdom (and indeed across most of the Western
world) family breakdown is now at epidemic levels. On current
estimates three million people (including children) are caught
up in the family justice system and every year another 500,000
get drawn into it. If family breakdown was a physical disease it
would undoubtedly attract emergency intervention and funding
by government. From time to time I have described it as a plague
or cancer or scourge that has insidiously infiltrated society over
the last 30 years. And, as we all know, it affects every level of
society, from the Royal family downwards.

The effects on children are in every sense profound and
permanent. They are affected by the experience, to a greater or
lesser extent, not only during their childhood but throughout
their lives. And the ripple effect goes far beyond the actual couple
and family. The effects are vertical in that they transmit both
up the family, to grandparents, and down the family to the next
generation and even beyond. But the effects are also horizontal.
Not only the wider family (sisters, brothers, aunts, uncles and
cousins), but also the community of which the family is part and,
ultimately, the whole of society are directly, and indirectly, affected
by this epidemic. It costs the country at least £46 billion a year,
which is a larger sum than the entire defence budget.

And yet despite the scale of the problem and the huge impact and significance in the lives of so many, the ignorance surrounding the whole subject is, quite frankly, both alarming and disturbing. The reason for that is, in the main, the lack of readily available and easily digestible information that covers all the important areas. Self-appointed social commentators who have frequently been through the experience, and so have strongly held subjective views (but no real knowledge or expertise), do not hesitate to offer advice or express often muddled and ill-informed views. Many of these castigate anyone who would dare to suggest that their children may have not relished exposure to the storm of parental separation. How dare anyone express a view! To do so, they say, is by definition judgemental.

But now, at last, we have this brilliant book. In a dispassionate, profoundly thoughtful and pellucid way a total expert tackles this multifaceted problem from every angle: emotional, scientific, psychological, practical and legal. With a subtle and powerful mixture of irrefutable hard facts, up-to-the-minute statistical detail and scientific research interwoven with poignant anecdotes and quotations from both adults and children, the entire canvas of family breakdown is surveyed in depth. The latest and most important new research around the neuroscience of child development is included, and by that route many modern myths (e.g. so called 'shared parenting') are tackled and exploded. In the end the great lie – 'I am so lucky my children seem to have come through unscathed' – is given a decent and timely burial.

But then, after the science and psychology, the practical, no nonsense, common sense advice (an attribute often lacking at the time of family breakdown) leaps out from the pages to help those tackling the tricky day-to-day problems inevitably thrown up by two parents living apart.

In the 1990s an attempt was made in parliament to reform appallingly outdated divorce laws by replacing the 1969 Divorce Reform Act with a new statute. The new statute required parents to attend an information session prior to filing a divorce petition to ensure they had at least the rudiments of knowledge of the pitfalls attendant upon splitting up the family. The act became law but has never been implemented or given a start date because it was said to be too expensive. So instead couples with children still, almost invariably, begin the process of separation (it is a very long process) ignorant on almost every front, both of the fallout to themselves and, more importantly, their children.

I would not be overstating the case if I said that this book should be obligatory reading for anyone even contemplating the ending of a relationship where children are involved. No, I would go further: it should be required reading for every parent, too. And it should also be read by politicians and commentators who presume to make policy or express views about this minefield of human behaviour. Indeed, dare I say it, every family judge at every level (from the court of appeal to the lay magistrate) should read, mark, learn and inwardly digest it to better equip themselves to make judgements in this sensitive field.

If there is any real chance of making inroads into this national problem we have to start with an informed and dispassionate debate based on hard facts and careful research, not personal experience, prejudice and moralising. The data is out there and the research exists, but it is often hard to find or interpret. This book solves both difficulties. It marshals, in a simple and straightforward manner, all the necessary material and presents it clearly and sensitively.

I wish I had had it 42 years ago. Both my professional and personal life would have benefitted immeasurably. I have it now and will read it over and over.

The Hon. Mr Justice Coleridge , High Court Judge Family
Division 2000–2014
November 2013

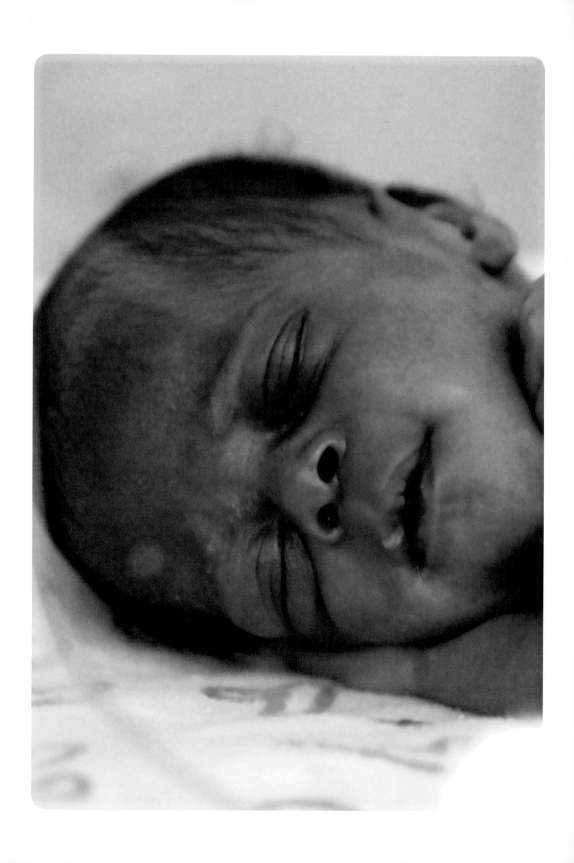

Introduction

If you are separating, divorcing or seriously considering it, you're not alone; you are not even in a minority. So many parents separate, whether from formal marriages, from civil partnerships or from cohabitation, that in the English-speaking world today fewer than half of all children celebrate their sixteenth birthdays with their parents still living together.

Tradition has it that marriage should last 'until death do us part', but in the modern Western world, where an average lifetime exceeds 70 years, it's often divorce rather than death that ends marriages. One third of couples who married in 1995 divorced before their fifteenth wedding anniversary in 2010. Half of those couples had a child or children under 16, two thirds of those children were under 11 and more than a fifth were under five.

Divorce statistics

Based on UK government statistics for 2010 it is estimated that 42% of all marriages end in divorce. The highest divorce percentages (well over 50%) are between the fourth and eighth years of marriage. That peak begins to drop around the tenth anniversary and slows further by the twentieth anniversary. The lowest percentages are amongst the longest-lasting marriages, 16% of which reach their sixtieth anniversary.

Analyses and predictions are complex because many factors affect them:

- **Partners' ages and any previous marriages**. On average, first marriages that end in divorce last about eight years. The median time between divorce and a second marriage is about three and a half years.
- **Wealth and sexual satisfaction** have been shown to correlate negatively with divorce rates in the United States. Richer and more sexually satisfied individuals are less likely to divorce.
- **Divorce is less likely if couples share a religious faith**. In a 1993 study in the United States couples who were each members of two mainline Protestant religions had a 20% chance of being divorced in five years, whereas a couple consisting of a Catholic and an Evangelical individual had a 33% chance and a couple in which one partner was Jewish and the other was Christian had a 40% chance. By 2001 marriages between people of any faith and those who attended church infrequently were three times more likely to end in divorce.
- **Higher education and age at marriage also correspond to longer-lasting marriages**. For example, of American college graduates marrying in the 1980s, 81% of those who wed when over 26 years of age were still married 20 years later, whereas only 65% of those who married under the age of 26 were still married 20 years later. In 2009, 2.9% of adults aged 35–39 without a college degree were divorced, compared with only 1.6% of adults in the same age band who had a college education

Figures from the UK Office of National Statistics

The social organisation of most societies in the West is still based on families, interlinked through marriage, although the statistics above make it clear that maintaining a good marriage against the social and sexual pressures and long duration of modern life is very difficult indeed. The only alternative that has emerged into social acceptability is cohabitation, which is not always very different from marriage and often precedes it. There is research – and political comment – suggesting that cohabitation is less stable and lasting than marriage. It is also suggested that having cohabiting rather than married parents is a disadvantage to children. In the UK in 2007, for example, 17-year-olds whose parents were cohabiting were less likely to remain in education than those whose natural (not step-) parents were married. Those findings, though, fail to distinguish between children who were planned within and born to cohabiting parents and unplanned children born to single mothers who later set-up home with someone who was not the father.

When a marriage ends so does the married couple's relationship, but when cohabitation ends it often becomes marriage. Getting married after a long period of cohabitation and the birth of children is increasingly common. For some couples such a wedding is a ceremonial, public celebration of the family they have made; children – and sometimes stepchildren too – often take part. For older couples, the main reasons for an eventual marriage ceremony may be legal and financial, perhaps to do with pensions and inheritance.

Marriage, cohabitation & birth statistics

The number of couples who marry is falling. In 1972 a peak number of marriages was registered in England and Wales: 480,285. By 2009 that figure had dropped to 231,490.

Couples living together, including same-sex couples linked in civil partnerships, are the fastest-growing family unit in the West. Numbers of cohabiting couples in the UK rose by 65% between 1996 and 2006, from 1.4 million to 2.3 million.

Forty-seven per cent of babies born in England and Wales during 2012 had parents who were not married. Of those, approximately 31% were registered to two parents living at the same address, 11% were registered to two parents living at different addresses while 6% were registered only to mothers.

The UK Office of National Statistics' most recent figures (2013) predict that by 2016 more than half of all babies will be born 'out of wedlock'.

Official figures for 2007 and 2012 from the *UK Office of National Statistics*

The dramatic fall in the number of couples who marry is largely due to changes in attitudes to sex, to marriage and to having children. In the 1960s and 1970s getting married was an intrinsic part of being recognised as an adult: it meant being able to have sex, live together and have children. That is no longer the case. People do all those things without first being married and according to the British Social Attitudes Survey conducted in 2008, almost two-thirds of people now see little difference between marriage and living together. Almost half of this large sample thought cohabitation showed just as much commitment as getting married. Furthermore, as the numbers of cohabiting couples increase and this form of partnership becomes socially normalised, research indicates that from children's point of view it need be no different from conventional marriage; only 28% of the British Social Attitudes Survey sample said they believed that married couples make better parents.

Whether they live together with or without marriage and whether or not they have children, it is clear that most adults seek committed partnerships. However, it is also clear that there are many individuals who cannot remain content for their whole adult life – 50 years perhaps – living with that one partner in a monogamous relationship that is a basic expectation of marriage or permanent partnership. There has to be a way that individuals can escape or move on, with as little damage as possible to themselves and to their extended families. And the way we allow for this, and what we increasingly choose, is divorce or separation.

Until a century ago, bad marriages had to be borne. In 1885 there were 300 divorces in England and Wales; in 1985 there were 150,000. In the United States the divorce rate in 2011 was almost twice what it was in 1960. It is only since the late 1800s that women have been legally allowed to sue for divorce with reasonable hope of keeping their children and their property. And even until the First World War a woman who left her husband, even if there was no other man on the scene, risked losing all contact with her children, as well as her 'reputation'. Marital separation was a disaster. There was no way to make the best of it.

Now separation and divorce, new partnerships, remarriages and step-parenting are such a big part of life for so many people, and so familiar to everyone, that it's difficult to believe that they are only a century old. Since being trapped in an unhappy marriage or forced to go through socially unacceptable divorce proceedings produced dreadful hardships for so many in the past, we should welcome the fact that divorce is now a well-established part of civil society via family law. However, it is one thing to welcome the existence of legal divorce, and perhaps press for it to be increasingly accessible, and quite another to welcome the actual process and its potential consequences.

At its worst divorce can still be bitterly antagonistic and even at its best it is very seldom pain-free, even for the partner who sought the separation. Being granted that decree may feel like liberation from a relationship that has gone sour or worse; if there is a new partner waiting in the wings it may even feel like the beginning of a new, exciting and romantic life. But even if the divorce works out well for one partner it will almost certainly be bad – emotionally and financially – for the other. And for a couple who have children, trying to spread the energy and the income that used to power one household between the two that now exist is horribly stressful, and so is the fact that however good the separation may be for both adults it will quite certainly be bad for their children.

Impact of separation & divorce on adult mental & physical health

In a random sample of 353,492 American adults, those who were separated or divorced had lower scores on the Well-Being Index which covers emotional and physical health, health behaviours, life evaluation, work environment and access to basic necessities. The managing editor of the think tank Gallup, Jeffrey Jones, calls these differences 'staggering'.

Life After Divorce.
Data measured by the Gallup-Healthways Well-Being Index, April 2012

In register-based data for 304,111 adult Finns, those approaching or experiencing separation or divorce were significantly more likely to use psychotropic medication (especially for depression). Following divorce there was excess mortality among males (though not females), especially attributable to accidental, violent or alcohol-related causes.

Metsä-Simola and Martikainen, 2013a, 2013b

Does that serious, even grim, message have a subtext suggesting that parents should stay together 'for the sake of the children'? No it does not. The more couples can be helped to improve their relationship to a point where they stay together because they want to, the better. But an unhappy partnership is unlikely to make for good parenting or happy children. And whether outsiders can understand the reasons for the break-up or not, parents (as opposed to childless couples) seldom separate or divorce lightly. Sometimes it seems as if they are doing so, as if they *could* have kept the relationship going if they had really tried, but it usually turns out that the immediate and seemingly trivial reason for parting (such as the boredom of the woman quoted below) is the final straw rather than the real cause. Separation is an event in a long process of family breakdown, and when that process is understood it usually shines a different light on what is best for the children.

Mother of three children aged 4, 6 and 9

> *I have a cousin in New Zealand and she's offered me a job in her own firm. No, my husband isn't coming. Yes, of course I asked him but he wouldn't dream of leaving his job and pulling up roots. But that's only his problem now, not mine. I've been bored out of my skull for a long time and this is a new start in a new country for me and the kids, with a job I can make something of for all of us.*

That may sound like a selfish decision, and, announced in this way to her husband and children it probably seemed like a bolt from the blue. In truth, though, it was a shaft of light out of grey skies. Absence of love, affection, shared goals or even everyday tolerance between parents leaves a chilly gap in children's lives whether they are eight months, eight or 18 years old. That kind of long-term dissatisfaction isn't as easily recognised as open parental irritation, depression or the sexual unfaithfulness, arguments, enmity and especially violence that poison many children's growing up. But if the long-term relationship between parents has gradually become joyless or intolerable to one or both of them it will not be a good environment for their children.

We have to accept divorce (and separation) as a safety valve for marriage and cohabitation. Adult society cannot do without one. But the wellbeing of children who will grow up to form that society in their turn is being put at risk by the way that safety valve is deployed. We can manage separation and divorce better. With children in mind, we should.

As people-who-are-parents you may divorce or leave one another but you cannot divorce and should not ever leave your children. As a family breaks up the needs of the children should be the adults' priority, not only for the sake of their current happiness and wellbeing but also for the sake of the people they are going to become in the future. It is everyone's good fortune that in this new millennium we know more than ever before about what those needs are.

Part I

When Parents Separate, What Makes a Difference to Children?

1 Seeing children's points of view

The break-up of a family isn't an event; it's a process and often a very long, slow one. Even if one partner has physically left, swearing that that's it, he'll have to be back. He'll come for his stuff, for more agonising conversations, rows and accusations, and maybe for some unexpected moments of nostalgic regret when the toddler holds up her arms to greet him. The parents nearly get back together again and he mows the lawn.

This is adult business at its most intense, and with this kind of stuff taking up most of your attention you won't have much to spare for anybody or anything else, including your children.

But this adult business is very much children's business as well. It may be your marriage that's breaking up, but it's their family. You are losing your husband, wife or partner, but they are losing not only the parent who is physically absent but both daddy and mummy, because even when you are present neither of you is the parent they had in the past. Deciding to separate has committed both of you to confusion in the present and, eventually, to finding new ways of life; your children had no part in the making of that decision and have no choice about what happens next. Your separation will turn your children's lives upside down and inside out. There's nothing you can do to prevent that, but if you recognise what's likely to make things better or worse for each child, then there is a lot you can do to moderate the storm.

Over 40% of UK marriages end in divorce. Divorce statistics like this make good shock headlines but focused as they are on divorce as adult business rather than on family breakdown, they tell us astonishingly little about children. That focus is wrong, both factually and morally. In the last two decades it has become clear that parental separation is very much children's business and that instead of being involved principally as weapons in marital war, they should be recognised as its victims. Family breakdowns are commonplace but that does not mean they are trivial – far from it. For children of all ages, from birth into adulthood, having the family split up is always deeply disruptive, usually sad and saddening and sometimes tragic.

Girl aged 10

When she was driving she just didn't seem to notice the lights changing so we all yelled 'lights' when we came up to a red one.

Boy aged 8

Dad came to see mum in the morning. Just mum. Not me. How do I know? Because he was surprised to see me home. He'd actually forgotten the holidays had started.

Girl aged 6

Mostly mummy doesn't hear me any more. She just says 'Mmm'.

Children with separated parents: satisfaction with life

The degree of satisfaction with life of 50,000 children aged 13, 14 and 15 with separated parents was compared with 150,000 children from intact families in 36 western countries.

Children in all post-divorce household types were less satisfied with life than children in intact families:

- Shared custody –.21 (least difference from intact families)
- Single mother –.28
- Mother and stepfather –.33
- Single father –.49
- Father and stepmother –.62 (biggest difference from intact families)

Nielsen, Fabricius, Kruk and Emery, 2012

The message that parental separation always makes children unhappy is not one that parents want to hear, so if it is mentioned at all it is usually only offered to them well-diluted with reassurances about children being 'resilient' and quickly 'getting over it'. For children's sakes, though, it is a message that needs to be widely broadcast and swallowed neat. Separating or getting divorced is a bad break for all of you and you need to face the fact that children are no more likely than you are yourselves to 'get over it' in the sense of forgetting about it or it ceasing to be important.

However willing you may be to face up to the impact your separation is likely to have on your children, you may not find it easy to get reliable and relevant information, because official statistics are mostly about divorce and are very inadequate sources. Not every divorce affects a child directly – in the UK about a quarter of divorcing couples are childless – and in those in which children are involved it will have been affecting them long before their parents actually get a decree and a place in the statistics. A great many children are affected by parental separations that never reach the divorce court, either because they are marriages which break-up without either spouse seeking divorce, or because they were parental partnerships which had no official rubber stamp at the beginning and therefore have none when they end. None of these appear in those statistics. Even when figures are given for divorces in which children are known to be involved, they tell us very little about those children. How many were involved per family or in total; their gender; their actual ages when divorce was granted; or even approximate ages when their parents' marriage began to disintegrate.

Statistics concerned with the proportion of families which
are single-parent are a little more child-focused, of course, but
their information is not straightforward because they seldom
differentiate between families in which the parents have
separated and those which have been single-parent from the
beginning or in which one parent has died. They do serve to
remind us, though, that many separations and divorces mean
many lone parents. There are around two million lone parents in
the UK, of whom 92% are mothers; 1.9 million lone parents each
have one child under 16; 621,000 have two children and 238,000
have three or more.

In more than 90% of single-
parent families the mother is
the lone parent and it is the
father who is absent. If it is
the other way around in your
case, you are in a minority
and a very small one at that.
It is often assumed that it is
mothers who end up as single
parents primarily because
men are more likely than
women to walk out on their
families, or because it is still widely assumed - by separating
couples themselves as well as by society and the family courts
that represent it – that it is more appropriate for mothers rather
than fathers to take daily charge of children. However, there are
even more basic reasons for the relative scarcity of lone-parent
men. Firstly, there is a far greater likelihood of early death amongst
males, so if a child has only one parent in existence it will probably
be his mother. Secondly, there is as yet no male equivalent to the
'unmarried mother', although with the use of donor eggs and
surrogates this may change.

Estimated proportions of families which have only one parent:

Australia: one in six

Canada: one in four

New Zealand: one in seven

South Africa: one in three

United Kingdom: one in four

United States: one in three

Compiled from *UNECE Statistical Database*

Statistics that tell us how many families were without one parent
tell us little about the reasons and rarely anything about what is
happening now, or will happen in the future, to the children within
those families. Indeed we cannot even be sure what 'family' means
or whether the way the term is used in one study is the same as
the way it is used in the next. Most people assume that 'family' is
about men and women having children together, but not every
family is based on heterosexual relationships. A growing minority
of children may be born to, or brought up by, a homosexual
couple who may be male or female and married or in a civil
partnership. A large majority of children are born to male–female
couples of course, but with no guarantee that that nuclear family
will be stable. For all children there is a considerable possibility

that their parents will separate and if they do their subsequent experiences are likely to be far more complicated than those simplistic statistical summaries suggest, because one or both are likely to form new partnerships. A parental divorce followed by even one lover per parent and one new spouse each makes four combinations of parent and parent figure, and each new combination may bring the child new grandparent, aunt or uncle and cousin figures, as well as step- or half-siblings, some of whom may be peers while others may be quasi-adults.

When you are thinking about what your separation will mean to your children it is important to bear in mind that children whose parents separate are liable to experience a complexity of relationships with adults in the remaining years of their childhood, and that these will change over time. Their parents may join up again, temporarily or permanently. Many couples go through several 'reconciliations' before the marriage is ended or, more rarely, reinstated. Children may live with their mother but have more or less close contact with their father. They may live sequentially only with their mother, with their mother and a lover or series of lovers, with their mother and a permanent partner or with their mother and a stepfather. Any of those men may, or may not, function as father figures for them, and any of them may, or may not, bring children of their own to form a melded family with yours. At the same time, the absent father may become the one they live with, and whether he does or not they may move through a similar set of relationships that may or may not bring them an extra mother figure and/or children who are formally or informally their stepbrothers and sisters. Eventually there may be half-siblings, too.

New families in old moulds

" *Once-nuclear families may re-form, once or several times, involving and excluding not only various parent figures and perhaps half or step-siblings, but also their relations. If a man comes to live with a divorced woman who has two children, does his mother become their grandmother? Can he, himself, be their stepfather if there is no marriage? If so, how long must he be in residence before he graduates into that role from being the mother's lover? And if there is a marriage, does he, the stepfather, remain part of the children's family if their mother divorces him? Modern Western families no longer fit the conventional nuclear family mold[.]* "

Leach, 1994

Making the best of a bad job

Nothing you can do will prevent parental separation from hurting your children but, thanks to research carried out in the past 15 years, parents who separate today (and their advisers) can do better by children than those of even one generation ago; better, probably, than your own parents did by you if they are separated. You can do better, and if you can you surely should. There is new and on-going research into children's development, especially their emotional and social development, that can help parents understand what their separation means to their particular children, and offers easily understood scientific information about ways of handling it that are likely to modify or curtail ill-effects.

We know how lastingly important family breakdown and parental separation is for children and we know some ways in which its impact can be minimised, right from the start. We know a great deal about what children and young people of different ages can be expected to understand about the separation and something about how to make it clear, day after week after month, that the separation is in no way the child's fault or a reflection of lack of love. Above all, we have real evidence to guide those difficult decisions about where and with whom children should live and how an absent parent can still be a mother or father. This kind of information, collected and delivered with the children's perspective always in the foreground, is badly needed because without it children may – and often do – suffer unnecessarily. When people say that it's 'only fair' for a father and mother to share the care of their five-year-old daughter on alternate weeks, they mean that it is fair to the adults – who see her as a possession and her presence as their right – not that it is fair to the child who needs a close relationship with both parents but also needs to *live* somewhere she can call home. And when a lawyer bids for his client to have his baby or toddler to stay overnight each weekend they are both ignoring clear evidence that such overnight separations from the mother are not only usually distressing, but also potentially damaging to the brain development and secure attachment of children under about four.

Information about children in separating families *in general* cannot be a prescription for your family in particular, of course, because every member of every family is unique and what works for one won't work, or be possible, for another. But there are now at least a few research-based dos and don'ts that seem to apply to all children of a particular age and in a particular circumstance. It will always be worth your while to think about such guidelines, which will usually be a much better bet for your children than having the two of you thrashing aimlessly about in small-hours arguments or taking contradictory chunks of advice from relatives and friends who have axes to grind and sides to take.

This kind of research will only really help you to help your children if you make a point of thinking about each child individually, and keeping them securely tucked away in a corner of your mind all the time, now and in the several years it will probably take before you all settle into new family structures. That is much easier said than done, especially while your own feelings and arrangements leave so little space for anything else, but it's the foundation of all the kinds of help that you can give them.

An 11-year-old girl, the middle child of three girls, was sent to boarding school because her furious father couldn't, and didn't pretend he wanted to, look after her and he would not allow her to live with her mother and mother's lover (her future stepfather). Her older sister escaped to drama school; her much younger sister was allowed to stay with mum. This child felt herself to be out of sight and out of mind.

The easiest way to preserve vital space in your head for everyone is to make a clear separation in your mind between woman–man and child–parent relationships (see Chapter 6). That means that you don't say (and try not even to look) the hurt, angry feelings that belong to your sexual relationship rather than your parenting. Your ex-husband may be a complete let-down as a husband; a hopeless provider; a faithless, insensitive man; a right bastard. But what is he as father to your child? Not 'ex' to begin with (the two of you may be getting divorced but he's not divorcing the child) and, given the chance, he's very likely not to be a let-down, faithless or insensitive either. One of the things that women who are separating often find most painful to accept is that their children still love the man they call daddy.

Working out how to share parenthood when you no longer share a household is often a personal and practical minefield – as we shall see in Chapter 7). But whatever the issues between you, and however you resolve them, now and in the future, do remember that you are both the parents of this child or these children, and that you are mother and father, not mother and (male) junior mother. You are different people in different roles and however you each fulfil your role, both of you are enormously important to your child.

Girl aged 11

My mum did write once a week, but lots of the other girls had letters and parcels and phone calls and visits... I told myself she was busy with her new life. I was glad for her. Yes, I truly was. I'd been so worried for her when she was so unhappy. But I felt I'd vanished.

A close relationship with their father is what matters

A review of research studies between 1987 and 2007 showed that children in intact families who had close relationships with their fathers did better in almost every way than those who did not. One study, for example, followed 8,441 infants to the age of 33 years and showed that those with closely involved father figures had higher levels of education and more close friends of both sexes and were less likely to smoke or to have had trouble with the police. Women who had had good relationships with their fathers at the age of sixteen grew up to have better relationships with their husbands and a greater sense of mental and physical wellbeing.

Lewis and Lamb, 2007

Recent British and American research has made a big contribution to our understanding of what parental separation means to children by not only studying families in crisis but also following the same families over a period of years. Thanks to this large and growing body of work we are beginning to accumulate what most of the research community would accept as 'facts'. Not every point may be true for your children, or the children with whom you are concerned, but taken overall these are the nearest we have to hard information.

- **Separation/divorce makes children miserable.** Children who are too young to understand what is going on between their parents often adamantly refuse to believe in the fact or permanency of a separation. Whatever you tell them, you will probably need to repeat it again and again.
  Older children who do understand that a separation is planned or permanent usually bitterly resent it. It seems clear that however poor the relationship between their parents has been, children would almost always prefer it to continue. Many dream of, and work for, reconciliation. The only exceptions researchers have found are among the few children who are physically terrified of the departing parent. They, and only they, may be relieved to see him or her depart.

These findings do not mean, of course, that a marriage which is not working should be held together 'for the children's sake' (children may be unwise in what they wish for), but the findings do mean that if you are separating you cannot assume that your children – even those who are almost grown-up – will agree that the family would be better split up than constantly quarrelling.

- **Children tend to take guilty responsibility upon themselves for their parents' break-up.** Younger children in particular, unable to fathom much of the reality of an adult sexual/habitual/co-operating relationship, tend to assume that they caused it to disintegrate. It is difficult for a child, whose whole life centres around his relationship with you, to realise that the same is not true of you: that swathes of his parents' lives are entirely separate from him. Furthermore, much of the friction that he has seen has probably involved his own behaviour – his noise or his discipline, his mother's spoiling or his father's neglect – so he easily sees these accumulated small issues as the cause of the crash.

There may be subtler reasons for guilt, too. Young children are sexually aware. In the normal course of early development they dream of partnership with the person of the opposite sex whom they love most (mother for a boy; father for a girl) and therefore fantasise about ousting the present partner (the other parent).

Boy aged 8, when asked, 'So what was the thing that made your daddy so angry?', answered:

Drinking my coke in bed.

The little boy who has secretly dreamed of 'looking after mummy' if only daddy didn't get in the way sees daddy's departure not only as a practical disaster but as evidence of his own wicked and terrifying power: he wished him away and now he wishes he had not. The little girl whose father leaves is similarly placed: clearly her love-object has left because it was wicked of her to want to get into her mother's place. The young child who is beset by this kind of guilt will be liable to separation anxiety too (see Chapter 8). Since her wickedness has caused one parent to leave the home, isn't it horribly likely that the other parent will also leave? At its mildest, such anxiety tends to make children cling to home and keep a too-careful eye on their mothers' movements. At the other extreme, it may make them feel so totally wicked and unlovable that they become convinced that neither parent can love them and that total abandonment is inevitable.

Older children, who have lived through the normal developmental stage of longing to replace the same-sex parent and have begun, instead, to identify themselves with him or her, are liable to a different sort of guilt. The separation makes them angry: angry, very often, with that same-sex parent. Whatever explanations they are given for the ending of the marriage they tend to feel (as do others outside the relationship) that they could have done better. A boy may feel that if he'd been his father he could have remembered to phone when he was working late, or could have spared one weekend day for the family; a girl may feel that if she'd been in her mother's place she could have held her tongue and avoided nagging. However justifiable that anger may be, it leads in turn to more guilt and to anxiety. Guilt over lack of sympathy with the same-sex parent and anxiety because if those real feelings were known, surely the parent who has stayed with the family would leave too.

- **Children tend to feel shut out by separating parents.**
  Most children, of all ages, crave attention from parents – often more attention than they easily get. The more involved parents are in couple-business the less attention they may be able to spare for parent-business. When separation actually takes place many parents (understandably) become so involved in their own feelings that they cannot remain engaged in children's everyday lives and cannot acknowledge the reality of their mourning for the loss of the absent parent.

Girl aged 13

> *You'd have thought she was the only one it mattered to. I just kept feeling: 'OK, I can see you're mis, but what about me?'*

To make matters worse, the parent who stays with the family is often as *emotionally* absent as the other parent is physically apart. Left with neither parent wholly with them, children feel unsupported and are aware that their own concerns are trivial as compared with all this high adult emotion.

- **Split loyalty is agony.** Children who suffer from it most are those whose parents make it acute by encouraging them to take sides. A few parents actually try to enlist children against their ex. Many more imply, often rather subtly, that any communication a child has with an absent parent is disloyalty (see Chapter 6).

While some conflict of loyalties is probably inevitable, a few of the points made by adolescents during interviews highlight the pain it can cause:

Boy aged 12

> *I couldn't bear him having to skulk on the street corner when he met us, but if he came to the house she looked all pained and long-suffering.*

Boy aged 16

> *Sometimes I'd say, 'Mum would have let me do such and such' and he'd say, very politely, 'If your mother had wanted to be the one to say what you should do, I think she'd have stayed around.'*

Girl aged 15

> *I wanted to phone him, tell him things that had happened, you know? She never stopped me; never said anything, but if she came in and I was on the phone to him she'd sort of go out, looking peculiar.*

Girl aged 13

> *She was unhappy, OK, I know that, but she was always sighing: over money or how hard she was working and all that. Every sigh and everything she said was sort of a dig at him.*

Boy aged 14

> *She'd ask me to do things, jobs around the place, and sigh because he hadn't done them before. I hated that; hated her for trying to make me feel I was better than him.*

- **Many children *worry* about the absent parent.** For young children in particular, exclusion from the warmth and safety of home and family seems a horrendous exile and the fact that dad left voluntarily is either beyond their comprehension or makes no difference to the fact that they worry about how he will manage alone.

Three- to ten-year-olds in particular ask:

Where will daddy sleep?
Who will cook his supper?
Who is looking after daddy?
Isn't he lonely? Doesn't he miss us?
Has he got a television? Will he watch Dr Who*?*

Mothers who share this kind of concern for the departed partner
(or can find in themselves the generosity to acknowledge the
reality of the child's concern) and can offer practical reassurance
that 'daddy's all right' do children an important service. As soon
as it is possible, children should see for themselves that the
father's living circumstances *are* 'all right'.

- **Children need parents to talk and to listen.** Research
  suggests that as many as one in five parents who are
  planning to separate are so flummoxed by the question 'what
  shall we tell the children?' that they tell them not much more
  than 'he's gone and good riddance'. Children whose parents
  discuss what is happening in the family with them and ask
  how it makes them feel not only survive the immediate shock
  better but also adapt more easily to the new circumstances.

Do your children know what's going on? Well, yes and no.
They probably know something's happening because daddy's
not living with the rest of you; they can see when you've been
crying; they realise Granny is furious though they are not sure
who with, and when the teatime fish fingers get burned and
there's no cereal left for breakfast three days running it's obvious
that their meals aren't claiming your attention. What they cannot
know unless you tell them is what it is that is happening and
why. Tell them. Trying to pretend that everything is just as usual
when it clearly is not will only increase their uneasiness and
sense of insecurity; and anyway, the fact that your separation is
long-term is not something you can conceal from them for long.
Once you have managed to tell them that mum and dad aren't
going to live together in the same house any more, do find age-
appropriate words to tell each child why. Telling them nothing is
not an option, because if you don't tell them why they will invent
reasons for themselves and their fantasies will probably be worse
than the reality:

Girl, now aged 11, looking back to when she was 5

She just said daddy didn't want to live with us anymore.
She didn't say why but I knew it was because he didn't
like me because I wasn't a boy and I still wet my bed.

The truth – perhaps that he, or you, have fallen in love with somebody else, or that he is more taken up with gambling than earning money for the family, or that you just don't love each other at all any more – may seem brutal, but half-truths or lies will eventually be exposed and then the children will have to face your untrustworthiness as well as the reality of what actually happened.

And there's another truth that you must give your children, however difficult you find it to say: both of you still love them. Whatever the circumstances, whatever hurt you adults have caused each other, that is between you and does not involve your children.

What you both say to your children is important, but what they say to you is equally so. Hearing and dealing with the pain your separation is bringing to your children can be so difficult that there is a temptation to brush aside their feelings about it, offering comforting words instead of a listening ear. Don't let yourself be tempted. Allowing, indeed helping, your children to express their anger and bewilderment, their fears and anxieties, will help them adjust to the new situation. And the more they can deal with their painful feelings in the here and now, the less likely those feelings are to bob up again and make emotional difficulties for them when they are older.

These conversations are not easy and there is no need to pretend that they are. Children can accept adult grief and anger and once they know what is happening, older ones at least, will expect you to be upset. If you can possibly manage it, though, don't make them feel that talking about the situation upsets you so much that they shouldn't mention it ever again, and try to make it clear to them that however hurt you may be you are not destroyed by what is happening. Somewhere inside each of you is a solid core of strength on which they can rely, now and always.

2 Children's ages & stages

Children's ages have powerful effects on how they perceive and are affected by parents separating and therefore on what they need from you both. If you have more than one child, each of them has reached a different age and stage of development from the others. Even if you have only the one, she is at a different stage today than three months ago and will be different again in three months' time. So while your family is imploding it's as important for you to try not to think or talk about your children collectively as 'the kids' or 'the boys' as it is for parents of twins to make a point of thinking and talking about the two children as separate people rather than as 'the twins'. These group references imply that everything that is going on is the same for all of them, which of course it is not. What is happening in your family will affect every child differently, so what you can best do to protect and support each one will be different too. Concentrating on each child as a separate person will help you to make sure that you understand, and meet, their different needs.

Mother of three children aged 3, 7 and 10

" The three-year-old has dropped all his most recent 'grown-up' stuff like using the potty. He's gone back to nappies and baby talk. The seven-year-old doesn't seem to care about her dad being gone; she's only worried about places and things: like will we have to move house and will we take the cats. As for the ten-year-old, she's ignoring both of us, really, and clinging to school and friends; she seems to be trying to be a teenager. "

Grandmother of a baby aged 9 months

" His dad keeps saying the baby can't understand a word of what is going on but I still wish they wouldn't count on him not knowing anything's happening. Words aren't everything and I can see him watching them both when they're arguing and noticing when his mum's feeding him his supper but really thinking about something else. "

Father of two children aged 17 and 19

" Our older kid is at uni and the younger one is having a gap year so I thought I'd waited long enough; they're too busy with their own lives to worry about ours. My ex says I'm dead wrong though. She says home still really matters to them and they're both really upset. "

Wishful thinking may make you inclined to underestimate the impact of your separation and the horrible strains that probably precede it, on your child or children, whatever their ages. However, research suggests that you are most likely to underestimate the upset of the two age groups at the extremes of childhood: babies and toddlers at one end, and teenagers and young adults at the other. It's much less likely that you will miss signs of unhappiness, bewilderment and anger in the age groups in between – primary school and early secondary school-aged children – because while they are often reluctant to talk about *what* is the matter, they usually make it all too clear that something is bothering them with noisy protests and 'difficult' behaviour at school as well as at home. Babies are different. As long as your baby is being adequately taken care of by familiar people in ways she is used to, she may seem unaffected by adult upheavals, or if there are signs of distress – such as lots of new night waking – it can easily be put down to that first molar coming through. Teenagers are different again; especially the post-16s who are at college or university. These almost-adult children who scarcely spend any time at home even if they are still technically living there may seem too taken up with their own relationships to be much concerned with their parents' relationship. Both of those assumptions are illusionary, though, and helping those youngest and oldest children through family breakdown depends on you being aware of that.

2.1 Babies

In human development, what happens in the future always depends on what has happened in the past. Your baby is at the beginning of her life and what happens to her now will lay the foundations for the whole of it. She isn't going to remain a baby for long, either. If she's a few months old when you decide that your marriage or partnership is at an end the chances are that she'll be a preschool child by the time things even begin to settle down, and how secure she is in herself and easy for you to relate to then will largely depend on what has happened to her in between. So even if it's your four-year-old who is wetting himself and resisting going to nursery, or your six-year-old who suddenly refuses to listen to a word you say and shouts back if you raise your voice, that apparently oblivious six-month-old needs at least as much of your thought and attention. If you both choose to accept that and act accordingly, fine. If you need some convincing here's a quick outline of the neuroscientific research findings that demonstrate its importance.

Do parents always know what children feel?

Recent research suggests that just as parents are inclined to overestimate their children's intelligence or how much exercise they take, so they tend to underestimate their children's unhappiness or anxiety – whether about parental separation or anything else. Special research materials were designed so that instead of relying on parents' reports of their children's feelings, children – between the ages of five and ten – could be asked directly about their emotional lives. The children's answers gave a much less rosy picture of their happiness and wellbeing than the answers given by their parents.

Lagattuta, Sayfan and Bamford, 2012

Why the first year is crucial

Brain development

Your baby, like all human babies, was born with an unfinished, still largely primitive brain. At birth he had only one quarter of the part of the brain whose eventual great size and complexity is what makes him human (the cerebral cortex). Three quarters must grow and develop from birth through toddlerhood: amazingly rapidly in the first year; still fast in the second year; and only a little more slowly in the third. Wherever he is in his first year, your baby's brain is an unfinished project and, like it or not, completing it is *your* project. He cannot do it for himself, it's down to you. His brain is going to grow, but how it grows and develops and functions doesn't only depend on the genes you passed on, or the physical circumstances and care you give him; it also depends on your feelings and behaviour towards him and the relationship that develops between him and each of you.

People have always known that babies' behaviour is affected by the way they are treated, of course. After all, that's the basis of all parents' attempts to encourage some behaviours and discourage others (smiling and hugging the baby when he is pleased and smiley; frowning and pushing him away when he grabs a handful of hair). But it's only in the last two decades that it's become clear that parents' behaviour towards a baby affects something far more basic and lasting than his behaviour right now: it affects the actual structure and functioning of that rapidly growing brain and therefore the kind of person and the way he will behave throughout his life.

Although the idea that how and whether you cuddle and comfort, play and talk with your baby permanently affects his brain is new and surprising, it makes very good sense once you've thought about it. Worldwide, babies flourish in a vast range of environments: from tropical forest villages to packed northern cities, from poverty and starvation to wealth and obesity and from secure adult affection to impatient rejection. Different environments and circumstances require different brain development, but babies can't be born with brains that are ready to fit in to any particular one of a myriad possibilities. If they were their skulls would have to be enormous: far too big for natural birth or for newborn neck muscles. So, instead of brains so large that they are ready for anything, babies are born with brains that are unfinished and adaptable to anything, which then grow with astonishing speed to make the best of the environment and circumstances in which they find themselves.

In the first days and weeks of life a baby's environment consists almost entirely of his mother, and his circumstances are hers. In fact, each baby in a newborn nursery is already somewhat fitted to the mother who carried and birthed him and he will immediately begin to adapt to her handling and their environment and go on doing so whether parents want him to or not. A new baby cannot wait in limbo while his mother recovers from the birth or his father arranges to start paternity leave. That's why premature or sick babies in special care baby units need to have parents close by as well as those vital specialised nurses. From the time of his birth a baby needs at least one particular adult who is devoted to him. If he has no such person, receives minimal or inappropriate adult attention, or arrives in a home that is a place of anger, strife or even violence, his brain structure and chemistry will immediately begin to adapt defensively. He may develop extra strong fear and anger reactions, or intense attack and defence impulses in the deep, primitive part of his brain. If, as the weeks pass, his brain continues to be suffused with stress hormones he may start to become hyper-vigilant, permanently prepared for 'fight or flight' and disproportionately upset by small things.

On the other hand, if a baby is born to a mother who celebrates her, cuddles and plays with her, listens to her, laughs with her and comforts her when she is upset, the connections that form in her brain will be very different. Because she can rely on an adult being available and aware of her feelings and ready to soothe and correct extremes of stress, fear and anger, she'll be on the way to becoming someone who can cope with emotional extremes for herself and form other close relationships with people.

Attachment

Everyone knows that babies need adult care every minute of every hour of every day and week, and it is obvious that a mother (or someone who stands in for the mother) with a close and loving relationship with her baby has the best chance of meeting the demands of constant caring without becoming bored or burning out. But while there is nothing new or remarkable about that, there is new evidence of how far beyond the provision of physical necessities and into the emotional world that care needs to go. When babies are born the left-hand 'thinking' part of their brains scarcely exists. The right side of their brains (and their newly separated bodies) experiences and reacts to deep primitive feelings: to fear, anger, excitement and misery. But they do not have the brain capacity to 'regulate' those fierce feelings, tone them down or bring themselves back from terror or excitement to calm. Unless somebody committed, and sufficiently devoted, keeps a check on the baby's emotional state, keeping him in mind even when he is not in sight, and lends him her own emotional resources, he may be overwhelmed. There are few more horrible sounds than the increasingly

hysterical crying of a young baby who is being ignored and left at the mercy of his own unmanageable feelings.

Attachment between a mother (it usually is the biological mother but it can of course be the father or someone else who stands in for her and may be referred to as 'primary caregiver') and her baby is a two-way street. The mother finds herself tuned in to her baby's feelings and those feelings – let's say fear – produce a reassuring response in her, which in turn produces a response in the baby, which she again picks up and reacts to. The two of them are a dyad: dancers, interdependent. The mother is attuned to the infant, keeping him always in her mind whatever else she is doing, and responding to him with her own right-brain responses rather than with conscious thought. Her attunement is helped by his instinctive behaviours and characteristics, such as clinging and sucking and eventually smiling. It is out of that attuned relationship that secure attachment grows.

Attachment is a survival mechanism. All human beings have an inbuilt genetic predisposition to seek refuge with whomever they are attached to when they are alarmed. People go on developing attachments all through their lives: to other family members, especially fathers; to adults from outside the family such as teachers; to childhood and adolescent 'best friends' and eventually to adult sexual partners. But the first attachment, forged in the earliest months of life to the mother or other 'primary caregiver', is the crucial foundation for all that follow. A baby or toddler who is securely attached can explore and experiment freely, provided the person who is his 'secure base' is available, or trusted to become available if he needs her. Her readiness to give any help he needs increases his sense of security and the assistance she gives models for him solutions to his current and future problems.

A very large, rapidly growing body of international research, which is undisputed though not yet widely understood, shows that babies' secure attachment to their mothers or whoever mothers them, and the attunement and responsiveness of mothers to their babies, is crucial to all aspects of lifelong development: to emotional stability and mental health and to physical health as well. Furthermore, stress, including the stresses that lead to and result from insecure or broken attachments, may damage a baby's capacity to learn and may, in extreme instances, damage it forever. When researchers compare children of any age on any aspect of development – learning language, resilience when things go wrong, sociable play with other children – the tuned-in-ness and readiness to respond of their mothers in the first year explains more of the difference between the children's achievements than anything else. It is a fact, not merely an opinion, that the more a baby experiences his mother or her substitute as attentive, responsive and loving, the more he will flourish today and the more resources he will have to cope with difficulties tomorrow.

Mothers, fathers & babies

Every human baby needs at least one special person to attach themself to. One is an absolute necessity and two are even better. All over the world the first special person (the 'primary caregiver' in research-speak) is more often the mother than the father. Pregnancy and birth set women up for the role, of course, but so does difference in the way female and male brains function. Taking the human species as a whole, females are better than males at understanding and responding to the communications of babies who cannot yet speak. Of course that does not mean that every woman is better at this than every man. Whatever the genders of a particular couple, one of them will probably take more easily to this role than the other. Within some male–female couples that may be the father rather than the mother, and, if circumstances allow, parents may organise their respective roles accordingly. Usually, though, the mother has the largest role and impact on the baby in the first year with the influence of the father – provided he spends enough time with the baby to exercise it – strengthening dramatically in the second year. This makes sense to attachment researchers who suggest that what babies need most in the first year is maternal reassurance and soothing while in the second year exploration and understanding of the physical world comes to the fore and is supported by fathers' more exciting, more challenging play.

If both of you shared your baby's care from the beginning, her emotional life will be both richer and safer for not being vested in one person alone, but that doesn't mean that you will be interchangeable so that if you split up the two of you can stand in for each other in your baby's life. However closely fathers are enmeshed in their lives most babies start out most relaxed of all with their birth mothers, perhaps due to long familiarity with their smells, heartbeats and voices, as well as to the bliss of sucking. More and more scientific research is showing how important the relationship between mother and baby is during the first months. For instance, findings show that it is the mother's loving responses to her during that period that raises the levels of the feel-good hormone serotonin in a baby's rapidly developing brain. If the two of them are separated, or a mother is too depressed or sad or angry to feel loving and to offer those responses, the baby's serotonin levels and her happiness may remain low.

By four or five months of age, babies with the luxury of two available parents will often play favourites. Fathers, rather especially fathers who have *not* been continually involved in their baby's routine everyday care, may suddenly find themselves singled out for favour because their sandpapery faces, deep voices and exciting play are new and interesting. But being flavour of the day doesn't make father into mother, or into a replacement for her.

Secure attachment to mother or a mothering-person is crucial to a baby's brain development and therefore to her whole future. Babies who don't have anyone who is really attuned to them, who perhaps receive efficient physical care but not much in the way of emotional response, or are looked after by a succession of caregivers, often do not develop as fast or as far as they might otherwise have done. And once a baby–mother attachment is underway, losing it, either partially or completely, always delays or distorts her development. If your marriage or your partnership is disintegrating while your baby is less than a year old, negative effects on her development are a real risk that you both need to be aware of.

However secure and reliable your relationship with your baby has been so far, and however determined you both are to protect her from the upheavals in your marriage, parental separation puts the mother–baby relationship at risk. You used to have a uniquely close two-way interaction with your baby without even thinking about it. But that becomes a struggle if your failing adult relationship keeps distracting you (see Chapter 5). And keeping your baby always in mind is a challenge when that mind is taken up with misery. There is even a risk that overwhelming adult problems and emotions may not only distract your attention from your baby but also put your attunement to her at risk. Being so much loved and needed may suddenly feel claustrophobic, so that instead of taking her dependence for granted you may find yourself yearning for at least a little time when she needs nothing from you. You may even feel that it is your relationship with the baby that has lost you your relationship with her father, and he may agree.

Fathers & mothers are different

Recent research shows that attachment to mothers and to fathers is qualitatively different. Secure attachment to mothers is promoted by the sensitivity of their care in the first year, whereas secure attachment to fathers is promoted by the quality of their play, and the way they support and gently challenge babies' and toddlers' explorations.

McIntosh, 2011

It is all too easy to let yourself assume that as long as she is being adequately looked after physically, that's enough, and then to fall back on going through the motions of mothering, or perhaps extra hours at nursery or even employing a caregiver. It isn't enough. You cannot build and maintain the security of your baby's attachment to you just by being her biological mother and arranging for her physical care. First love is not cupboard love. Your baby doesn't just need a caregiver to come and feed or change her when she's hungry or wet, she needs someone who bears her constantly in mind and comes when she is bored or lonely or uncomfortable; someone who notices when she smiles and smiles back, who hears when she 'talks' and listens and replies; somebody who plays with her and shows her things, bringing little bits of the world for her to explore. If you always do all those things anyway, you may be surprised to hear them described as 'important'. You are so attuned to her that these are not things you think about but simply things that you do, 'action without thought' in response to a baby whose thinking brain is not yet developed. If so, all well and good. These are the things that really matter to your baby. Sadly, though, they are the very things that are likely to be put at risk by an adult relationship tsunami.

Mother of boy aged 8 months

" I'm trying really hard to keep everything the same for him. Like I take him to the playground every afternoon but the minute I start pushing him in the baby swing I start daydreaming. In fact yesterday I went on pushing him longer than he wanted and didn't realise he wanted me to stop until he was actually crying. I felt awful. But then a friend came later in the afternoon and I put a DVD on so we could talk, just for a minute, only we went on talking so long that he dropped off to sleep and he hadn't even had his tea. "

Mother of two girls aged 6 months and 4 years

" Jemima's four and she's getting louder and louder. Everything she says is a shout or a yell and the more I tell her to hush the worse she gets. The only person she talks normally to is baby Jess. When I asked her why she said 'Cause you can't hear us you only listen to the people on your phone.' "

Father of two children aged 11 months and 3 years

" We were having supper like we used to do; round the kitchen table; normal family stuff. I was helping James with his food and my soon-to-be ex and I were talking. It got a bit tense and then suddenly James shut his mouth and turned his head away and wouldn't eat… it was as if he was angry. I think he was angry. "

Baby-sharing

When a marriage or partnership breaks down there's a lot of sharing out to be done but don't make the mistake of confusing sharing out objects or money with sharing out people and relationships. You cannot make up to your baby for less attention from you by arranging for him to have more from his father or vice versa. 'Shared parenting' (see Chapter 7) has nothing to do with your separation and is not a solution to the stresses of this time. You don't share the parenting of your children because you are parting, but because you are both their parents: always have been and always will be.

Unless parents 'reversed roles' early in this first year, the mother is the primary parent and, right now, hard though it may be for the father to acknowledge, her relationship with the baby is even more important than his. Whatever is going on in their adult relationship, it is essential to the baby that both parents have a real understanding of the vital importance of her relationship with her mother and of the importance these months of being mothered will have to the whole of the rest of her life. All the developments and milestones of this first year are waiting inside her. She has a built-in drive to master and practise every aspect of being human, from making sounds, using her hands and rolling over, to eating real food or sharing jokes. But the achievement of each aspect of her growing up is also in the hands of her mother or whoever stands in for her. The more that primary caregiver holds and plays and talks and sings with her, keeping her on track, balanced, interested and busy, the more completely she will fulfil her potential for brain growth, development and learning: her potential as a person. This is no time to be arguing about fair-shares as if she were a meal that could be divided so as to feed you both. By all means agree to share your baby's parenting through and beyond your separation, but make sure you are both clear that what you will be sharing is not the hours of her physical presence or care, but your love and concern and responsibility for her.

First attachment: the primary caregiver

> *To my mind there is one single 'primary' caregiver. A good definition of the primary caregiver is that, under stress, the baby moves towards this single person in order to seek the external regulation he/she needs at the moment. Under stress, the baby will usually turn to the primary caregiver, not the secondary caregivers. In most family settings, things are building with the father in the first year and he is definitely getting a good sense of who the baby is, but the primary bond in most cases is to the mother in the first year and then, in addition to her, to the father and others in the 2nd and 3rd years.*

Babies' attachment hierarchy

> *[…] my read of the current research is that the child's first bond is to the primary caregiver's (the mother's) right brain. At a later point, the 2nd year, the child will bond to the father if he is also providing regular care. At this later point, separation from the father will also elicit a stress reaction from the baby, the same as it would with separation from the mother. The second attachment and separation reaction is thus occurring at a later point in time than it would for the mother. Expanding upon these ideas I've suggested that although the mother is essential to the infant's capacity for fear regulation in the first year, in the second the father becomes critically involved in both the male and female toddler's aggression regulation.*

Schore and McIntosh, 2011

Fathers, mothers & toddlers

Acknowledging that being with her mother is more important to their baby than being with him is one of the most difficult things a loving father facing the break-up of his family needs to do. It's as important and as difficult as it is for an angry, perhaps betrayed and deserted mother to acknowledge that the children still love their daddy. If you want your separation to hurt your baby as little as possible though, you do need to accept the growing body of research clearly establishing that in the first year of life this is so. It takes true selflessness for a father to put his baby's feelings, and his soon-to-be ex's ability to meet them, ahead of his own, but if you can accept the research evidence that you are likely to be second rather than first-in-line for your baby's first attachment hierarchy, further research will reward you with evidence of the growing importance of father–child relationships as babies enter toddlerhood, and the overall and lifelong benefits to children, adolescents and adults of long-term relationships with fathers.

Three further sets of observations – and your own common sense – may further help to strengthen your resolve:

- The better father and baby know each other in her first year, the closer the bond between them will be in the second year and later. If you want the closest possible relationship with your toddler, don't go off in a huff because right now she's still a baby and loves mummy best.
- Forming a secure attachment relationship with your baby and maintaining it when she is a toddler doesn't depend on her spending whole days or overnights or weekends with you. It doesn't even depend on her spending time with you that is right outside her mother's orbit. The two of you can become securely attached just by spending enjoyable and predictable daytimes together. That, after all, is what the close attachments that often develop between grandparents and very small children are usually based on.
- If you are trying to make or strengthen your attachment relationship with your child, forcing her to leave her mother and go with you, whether it's for an afternoon or a weekend, is completely counterproductive for you as well as cruel to her. If she cries and clings and eventually has to be passed over like a parcel or peeled off her mother and into your arms, what she will remember is not the nice time she eventually had with you but the distress of that parting. Next time a visit comes up she will be even more distressed, not because of anything you did or failed to do, certainly not because she does not, in her own infant terms, love you, but because she's reminded of her own painful feelings last time and anticipates feeling that way again.

Babies, toddlers & shared care

Since the late twentieth century, the enormous importance of fathers in children's lives has been increasingly recognised and a growing – though still relatively small – number of men have become actively involved in hands-on care of their children within marriage, and anxious for arrangements to share care after marriage breakdown (see Chapter 7). Many of the professionals who work with separating couples consider that as long as both the mother and father are willing and able to look after the children, arranging for each of them to share in the children's care serves both adult justice and child wellbeing. Indeed there is a presumption in family law in the English-speaking nations that parenting should be shared equally after family separation (see Chapter 4.5). The underlying argument, vociferously supported by Fathers' Rights organisations in the UK, is that this is the only way to make sure that fathers remain an integral part of their children's lives after parents have separated.

Even when parents are anxious to co-operate with each other, however, equal shares of children's time and care are rare. Fewer than one in ten children are based with fathers rather than mothers and most children spend more time with their mothers than with their fathers. For children of school age the geography and the timetabling of their school lives usually have a major impact on shared care arrangements (see Chapter 4). The practical potential for more or less equally shared care is greater for younger children – for babies, toddlers and preschool children – than for older children and this is unfortunate. Since the mid-1990s, a great deal of research regarding parental separation and these younger children has been carried out, principally in Australia and in the United States. Findings strongly suggest that shared care that includes spending nights, or even a single night at a time, away from 'home' and mother is seldom in the best interests of children under around four years of age irrespective of the families' socio-economic background, their parenting or the co-operation between the parents.

Impact of shared care on babies & toddlers

- Babies and toddlers under two years of age who spent one or two nights a week with a non-resident parent were more irritable than children who were primarily in the care of one parent, and were also more watchful and wary of separation from that primary caregiver.
- Children aged two to three years who spent five or more nights a fortnight with a non-resident parent showed significantly lower levels of persistence with routine tasks, of learning and of sociable play than children who were primarily or entirely in the care of one parent in one place.

- The extreme attachment distress of regularly separated toddlers could be seen in their relationships with the primary parent. Some became very upset, crying or clinging to the parent; others became aggressive, hitting, biting or kicking. A few developed eating problems such as food refusal or gagging
- No ill-effects of being 'time-shared' between parents were evident in children past their fourth birthdays

McIntosh, 2011

Of course not every child under four who spends some nights away from her mother will show ill-effects, but unless the mother is actually incapable of caring for the child full-time so that the only alternative is extended family or foster care, it is doubtful whether any child in this age group will actually benefit from spending some nights with one parent and some with the other.

If you are thinking about, or struggling with, shared care that includes overnight stays for your baby or toddler these are warnings to be heeded. Asking yourselves and each other the questions below may help you to decide whether or not this particular child is likely to be able to tolerate moving between two parents and flourish in two homes.

Who is this child?

- *How old is she?* A three- or four-month-old baby may not be obviously distressed by separation from mother into father's care as her attachment to mother is not yet fully formed and exclusive. However, while such a young baby may not be visibly upset there is a serious risk that frequent separations will disrupt her primary attachment to her mother and its security. Taking childhood as a whole, older children sustain separations better than younger ones, but this is not the case in this youngest age group where two- and three-year-olds appear to be especially vulnerable.
- *What sort of person is she?* Is she easy-going or anxious? Sociable or shy? Easy or difficult to comfort once upset?
- *Is there an older sibling who will be transferring with her from one home to another?* Overnights appear to be easier for young children when they have an older sibling going with them to ease the transition (see Chapter 3.1). Be careful, though. While the bond with an older sister or brother may be an important support to the younger child, being expected to be supportive may be an added burden to the older sibling.
- *What sort of relationship does the child have with each parent?* The more securely she is attached to at least one of you – say her mother – the better she will be able to cope with spending time with her father, provided that he can provide warm, responsive care. If the child is securely attached to both parents and readily turns to each of you for comfort, then she should be able to switch between you relatively easily. On the other hand, if father and the child are not securely attached to each other and she does not confidently turn to you for comfort or reassurance when her mother is not there, overnight stays will be inadvisable and extremely stressful.

- *What were the parenting arrangements for this child before the separation?* If one parent has always been the primary attachment figure while time with the other parent has been sporadic or disrupted or even non-existent, only limited, brief, daytime visits should be attempted until a secure relationship has formed.

A baby's or toddler's happiness and security in a divided family and two homes is not down to her, of course, it is down to you – and is by no means easy to achieve. Whatever she is like as a baby personality, and however ready she may seem to be to use a secure attachment to her mother as the basis for security with her father also, the success or failure of shared care in two homes depends on how each of you feels and behaves, separately and together.

What kind of parents are you?

- *Do each of you have a secure and warm relationship with the child that predates your separation?* If your fathering was formerly hands-off, you cannot hope to transform yourself overnight into a secure attachment figure and competent practical parent; it will take time and practice. Equally, if your mothering was mostly confined to after-work 'quality-time' and otherwise supported by a live-in nanny who can no longer be afforded, you and the child both face unimaginable upheaval, separately and together.
- *Are both of you genuinely supportive of each other's relationship with the child?* If you want her to be equally happy and secure with each of you, you'll both take endless care to be positive and reassuring to her when she's transferring from one of you to the other (see Chapter 5.1).
- *As a non-resident father are you confident that you can maintain your child's consistent and predictable routines while she is staying with you?* That means knowing what and how and when she eats, plays, bathes and sleeps, which cuddly animals or other comfort objects share her bed and which songs or stories end her day. Even if you were a hands-on participant father who knew every detail of his child's life until you moved out of the family home a few months ago, those are not details you can take for granted. Children grow and change and at this stage in their lives they do so amazingly fast. Since you last put your daughter to bed Pink Piggy may have made way for Dragon.
- *Is your relationship with your ex conflict-free?* If conflict should arise, you should both be determined to ensure that it does not take place within sight or hearing of the child.

- ***Do both of you monitor and discuss the child's reactions to the separations?*** If either of you should run into problems, even in the middle of the night, you should feel able to telephone for the other parent's advice.

Unless you can both come very close to meeting these ideals your child will be better off if you make arrangements for sharing her parenting that do not involve her in spending nights away from home, at least until she approaches school age.

2.2 Toddlers & preschool children (18 months to 4 years)

Even if they are not expected to divide their time between two parents and homes, children between, say, 20 months and rising-five usually react to parental separation with a mixture of grief and rage. And although the older children of any other age group tend to cope more robustly than the younger ones, that is not the case here. It is often children around the age of three who react most negatively.

Early toddlerhood is a stage of development when all children, even those in the most secure and predictable families, tend to suffer from 'separation anxiety': the fear of being lost by, or of losing, a parent. At this age your child's brain is only just becoming able to hold onto an image of you when he can't see you, and therefore he is only just beginning to understand that when you go away you still exist and will come back. In the meantime he naturally wants to keep an eye on you and to go with you wherever you go. If you want two minutes privacy in the bathroom you have to pick your moment or put up with him thundering on the door.

When one parent – let's be realistic and say daddy – moves out and is no longer there to do the parenting things he used to do, like read the bedtime story or help with dressing in the morning, he really is lost to the child. Lots of visits in the daytime over the next months, combined with his brain's maturing, will gradually help the child to believe in his vanishing father's continued existence and to have confidence in his reappearances, but in the meantime he will probably experience daily life as a miserable muddle especially as, having lost daddy, he is desperately anxious about losing mummy (see Chapter 8.1).

Whether your toddler is a boy or a girl, he or she is likely to cry far more often and for longer than before and to be extra demanding of adult attention. If the child is a boy, he may suddenly seem to become both angry and restless as well as sad. Don't be surprised if teachers at nursery tell you that he withdraws from his former friends, spending a lot of time sitting alone, and that when he does join in group activities he is 'difficult' and disruptive. Some girls react to parents separating in a similarly sad and angry way, but other girls cope completely differently. You may find yours suddenly behaving like a very small adult, trying to take care of herself instead of seeking adult help, and perhaps becoming worryingly concerned with being 'a good girl' and keeping her clothes clean.

Insecurity, anger and sadness make a potent mixture which, in a large enough dose, can slow up, halt or even reverse the most recent and 'grown-up' developments of this not-quite-baby-not-yet-child age group. Newly dry beds may be wetted again, the toilet rejected in favour of a nappy. Demands may be made for help with eating, for milk in a bottle rather than a mug, or for a dummy, and whenever you go out there may be endless requests to ride in the buggy or be carried, rather than walk. Your child demands more of you just when it would be easier for you if you could give less. And if you do give less – because you can't help it – the demands will escalate.

Even under the most peaceful family circumstances adults often find toddlers and preschool children difficult to live with, and the circumstances of family breakdown are far from peaceful.

Learning how to behave

> *Children are noisy, messy, untidy, forgetful, careless, time-consuming, demanding and ever-present. Unlike even the longest-staying visitor they don't ever go away. They can't be shelved for a few weeks when you are extra busy, like a demanding hobby; can't even be ignored, like pets, while you have a Sunday lie-in because they have an unfailing ability to make you feel guilty. The guilt-trips that come with children are worse than the upturned cereal bowls, bitten friends or walls drawn on with lipstick. Loving children (as almost every parent does) magnifies the pain of them as well as the pleasure. Loving them may even make it difficult for you to admit that they are sometimes a pain.*

Leach, 2010a

Do try your best to stay on her side. Although she can understand what 'no' means and recognise when you are cross with her, she doesn't yet understand *why* you approve and disapprove of particular behaviours and that means that she is nowhere near ready to cope with your anger or disappointment or sadness when she doesn't co-operate. If you are angry with her she will certainly be upset, but she won't learn anything useful from it because the reasons for adult feelings and behaviour are still a complete mystery to her, so your anger seems to her as meaningless but terrifying as a thunderbolt.

Between two and three, a growth spurt may mean that she suddenly looks more like a child than a toddler but the saddest mistake you can make is to think of her, or treat her, as more grown-up than she actually is. Above all, don't let yourself expect her to understand that you are having a tough time and need her to be 'good'. If you and she keep quarrelling, think through the last occasion – breakfast perhaps – from her point of view rather than from your own. She didn't know – couldn't know – that spilling her mug of milk so it splashed the sleeve of her sister's clean school shirt was the 'last straw' on a really bad morning. She didn't know that it was a bad morning or what that means. If she sensed anything at all as you raced around the kitchen, late and multitasking, eyes still swollen from last night's tears, she will only have sensed your general tension, and although she will have disliked it, she will neither have understood what it was about nor even wondered. She doesn't understand much about your feelings or your life because she hasn't had enough experience yet and the part of her brain that enables empathy is only now developing.

It may be helpful to realise that the difficulty you are having in coping with a child in this age group when you are already highly stressed is not due to her bad behaviour but to your general irritation with her childishness. It will help the child because if she cannot be childish when she is two or four years old, when can she be? It will help you not to decide that she is especially disobedient, ill-disciplined and spoiled, and therefore blame yourself for being a bad parent – which is the biggest guilt trip of all. And it will remind everyone who ever has any contact with your child – from grandparents to nursery school teachers – not to stick onto her the problem-labels that so easily become self-fulfilling prophecies. If your child believes that you or her father think she is naughty and nasty, she will live up to that view and probably come to share it herself, and make sure that her teachers do too. So try to hang onto the truth, which is that she is very young, that family life is especially difficult right now, that you aren't perfect and shouldn't expect yourself to be, and that things will change for the better. You can count on that because the one thing that's certain is that your child is going to grow older, easier to communicate with and more able to understand.

2.3 Infant/primary school-aged children (4 to 7 years)

School-aged attachments

Many children behave very differently with parents in their homes and with unrelated caregivers elsewhere, and the nature of their attachment relationships with the adults in each setting will usually be part of the explanation. By school age, though, most children have arrived at one dominant style of attachment which applies in all their relationships, so that 'a shy child' will be noticeably shy in all settings while a secure child will take his confidence with him wherever he goes.

Leach, 1994

Many rising-five- to seven-year-olds do seem to react to family breakdown differently from children who are a year or two younger or older. In both sexes the main reaction at this point is often sadness alone, without the anger younger children often display. Many teachers (and even classmates) report that these children are 'always crying' and when they are asked what they are crying about they usually answer straightforwardly 'I miss my dad' or 'I want my mum to come home'.

But the crying is unlikely to be only about missing a parent. These children are overwhelmingly sad because they assume that a parent who has moved out of the shared family home has rejected them. Many in this age group are mature enough to seek an explanation for the parental break-up but only the exceptional child will look in the right place – the relationship between the parents. Almost all will assume that the whole horrid upheaval is their fault. Daddy has gone to live somewhere else because they are unlovable and unloved.

As well as blaming him or herself for the parent's absence, and missing him or her, your child may also be deeply worried about both of you and will almost certainly be desperately hoping to get you back together again.

Boy aged 4

My daddy does the long grass 'cause mummy can't. He washes his hands and last time he had a cup of tea. But then he wented again.

Boy aged 7

There's a concert at school and I'm IN IT so this time they'll both come and they'll sit next to each other and then we'll all come home together

Girl aged 7

When the phone rings I always think it'll be daddy coming home.

Boy aged 5

It's cause I woke up too early . . .

Boy aged 7

I talked too loud. He always said 'hush' and I didn't

Girl aged 8

They didn't want to get me from school. I heard them yelling about having better things to do.

Girl aged 7

That was my nearly-asleep dream, about dad coming up the path with his wheelie and mummy giving him a big hug.

If your child is feeling like this there is a real risk of depression and a high probability of a drop in performance at school and in any after-school activities. Boys in this age group whose fathers leave home are likely to be even more distressed than girls however regularly fathers visit, and there may be complaints about their behaviour at school, adding to their feeling that they are bad boys whom nobody loves.

2.4 Primary school-aged children (8 to 11 years)

If sadness is the predominant emotion in most rising-five- to seven-year-olds whose parents separate, anger often overwhelms it in this age group. Your child may be intensely angry with one or both of you during and after the break-up of the family. He or she is likely to take sides against whichever parent is seen as having fractured family life, often seeming to take pleasure in apportioning blame. Very often, of course, a child's limited understanding of the situation means that he or she blames the wrong parent. You may discover that your son blames you for forcing his father to leave the family home when the reason you took a stand was an ongoing affair. Unfortunately their interest in which parent was at fault makes children in this age group especially vulnerable to parental blame-and-revenge games (see Chapter 6).

However angry your child may be, though, anger will not be his or her only reaction to the family upheaval. Although people often describe children as self-centred, egocentric and selfish, many children in this age group are also enormously concerned for their parents wellbeing, frightened about what is going to happen to them and lonely for the people they used to be. Even at this young age many also try to take care of the parent with whom they are living, acting like parents themselves and trying to make things better for the adult.

More than anything else in the world, most children want the family breakdown not to have happened or, failing that, for their parents to get back together again. But however passionately they want things to change they are powerless to change them and, deep down, they know they are. Furthermore this is an age when children's social lives and their desire to conform to the peer group are becoming increasingly important. Should they tell their friends about the parental separation? What will they think? And if they don't tell, how can they explain why Saturday's sleepover and their June birthday party are at different addresses?

Girl aged 10

When we're at school she's all by herself. Nobody to help her with stuff, go to the shop for her or answer the phone. OK my dad was at work but he was coming home. Now he isn't. She doesn't cook supper like she did and I don't know what she will do.

Boy aged 9

He hasn't got a proper house or his garden or his shed. He's just got a little room and he's all alone in it with nothing to do and nobody to talk to. Mum says not to worry he'll just be in the pub but I don't think she means it nicely.

Confiding in peers

Findings from research based on data from longitudinal studies, such as the National Institute of Child Health and Human Development Study of Early Child Care and the Minnesota Study of Risk and Adaption from Birth to Adulthood, consistently show that the security of children's early attachment relationships are predictive of their peer relationships later on. Children who have been securely attached since early infancy tend to have more and closer friends than insecurely attached children, and are less likely to dislike or be disliked by others.

Crittenden and Claussen, 2000

Children want to be in control of who-tells-what-to-whom but they are unlikely to be able to manage it for themselves.

If you are on friendly terms with the parents of your child's best friend or friendship group, offer to tell them what is going on so that they can tell their children. As for the school: the head teacher and school secretary need to know about the separation so that communications from the school are sent to each of you. But in addition, unless the child is strongly opposed to the idea, it will probably be helpful to talk to her class teacher who is the adult best placed to keep a supportive eye on her and cut her a little slack when necessary.

Girl aged 8

I want Amelia to know I'm sad but I don't know what to say to her. 'My dad's gone' sounds really weird. It is weird actually.

For children in this age group there is about a fifty–fifty chance that his or her school performance will drop-off alongside self-confidence and ability to concentrate. As in younger age groups, boys are more susceptible than girls both to becoming withdrawn and to 'acting out' their feelings in unacceptable behaviour. Children of either sex may also react to the complex web of emotional distress family breakdown causes with psychosomatic symptoms such as headaches and bellyaches. These are not 'made up'; the pain is real, but its basic cause is emotional rather than physical. If psychosomatic complaints are a major feature of a child's reaction to the family breakdown a visit to a (sympathetic) GP may be helpful, because the child herself may be worried about her health and welcome reassurance that her symptoms are caused by sadness and stress rather than illness.

2.5 Secondary school-aged children (11 to 16 years & upwards)

Transferring from primary to secondary school is stressful for most children when home and family is stable, and for every child when the family is in crisis. Although your 13-year-old's concern over the situation may be less obvious than your nine-year-old's, it will probably be even more intense and potentially more hazardous.

Brain development in the teen years

There is overwhelming and still accumulating neuroscientific evidence that highly significant brain development takes place during adolescence, especially early adolescence – under 13–14 years. The key aspect of this is the marked immaturity of the neural networks of frontal brain regions implicated in planning, perspective taking, social understanding and evaluating future consequences. The brain immaturity manifests in impulsive decision making, decreased ability to consider long-term consequences, engagement in risky behaviours and increased susceptibility to negative influences.

Specifically, this body of research indicates that early adolescence marks the onset of puberty, heightening emotional arousability, sensation seeking and reward orientation; that mid-adolescence is a period of increased vulnerability to risk taking and problems in affect and behaviour; and that late adolescence is a period in which the frontal lobes continue to mature, facilitating regulatory and executive competence.

Casey, Jones and Hare, 2008

Adolescence is a stressful period of development and how your adolescent child reacts to the added stress of family breakdown depends not only on chronological age but also on the point he or she has reached in the development of puberty. Bear in mind that immature brain development means that teenagers tend to be emotional, impulsive and liable to take risks without thinking through consequences.

Some adolescents who don't like what is going on at home partially disengage from their families and spend more time with their friends elsewhere. This can be a good adaptation or a risky one, and only you two can decide which is the case with your child. For a 14- or 15-year-old who has already achieved some personal autonomy and independence from his parents, effectively focusing on his own ambitions and plans and disregarding the parents' problems may be an adaptive way to react to family breakdown. But when a 12- or 13-year-old who feels lonely without the accustomed family structure and is less carefully supervised than before (see Chapter 9.2) takes refuge with groups of somewhat older peers, there is a real risk of him or her joining in with exciting risky activities often involving underage drinking, sexual activity or drug-taking possibly coupled with shoplifting or other antisocial or illegal behaviour.

An opposite reaction, seen almost exclusively among girls, pulls a teenager more closely into the family, coping with her own loneliness, confusion and guilt by helping to run a fractured household or care for younger children.

If you are struggling to work full-time as a single parent your adolescent's willingness and competence may be crucial. But if she is expected to provide tea and sympathy for younger schoolchildren and perhaps to complete the day's domestic chores and prepare an evening meal, do acknowledge that in enabling you to do a full-time paid job she is doing a part-time one herself. She is in exactly the same position as she would be if she worked in a family business.

It can be very valuable to an older adolescent to feel that he or she is a necessary part of the home set-up, but don't let yourself slip into dependence on her labour. There will come a time when he or she wants (and needs) either to leave home altogether or to transfer to 'lodger' status while attending college or serving an apprenticeship. It is one thing for the adolescent to feel needed, quite another to know that his or her presence is literally indispensable. When he or she leaves school and finds a job, you must not ask, even silently and with your eyes, 'who is to look after the little ones until I get home from work?' That must not be the adolescent's problem, because it is yours. You need to have foreseen both question and answer in advance. Leaving home is difficult enough for many youngsters without that kind of added stress.

In the meantime, however welcome her help and companionship may be, don't often let her stay at home instead of going out with friends or help small siblings with homework instead of doing her own. It is not her job to manage your problems; it is your job to protect her from them.

Many of the dilemmas and difficulties that are normal in families with teenage children are exacerbated by parental separation. Even in intact and stable families, for example, many adolescents of all ages and both sexes experience conflict between home life and peer group life. If most of every weekend goes on sport the young person may see very little of his or her family; and if every Friday and Saturday night is for going out with friends, he or she will be left out of family birthday celebrations or treat dinners. Balance and compromise is needed.

When parents separate, the need for that balance is doubled but available compromises are often halved. Arrangements that ensure a child spends time with each parent – such as weekends with dad – may work well when children are in primary school but become intolerable to teenagers who need to be allowed, even encouraged, to stick around and hang out with their friends. But at the same time that they are fighting against having to be away from home base every weekend, many adolescents will regret seeing less of the non-resident parent and feel guilty for not doing more to fill the empty partner-shaped space in each parent's life. Boys may feel that they ought to be 'the man about the house', not only in the sense of changing light bulbs or carrying heavy stuff but also in the sense of looking after their mother if she seems sad or lonely. Girls likewise often feel obligated to keep their fathers company. Sometimes such relationships become inappropriately romantic, even seductive, unless parents draw and maintain very clear lines between adult and child, parent and friend.

2.6 Students & young adults (16 to 18 years & upwards)

The depth of the effect parental separation or divorce can have on 'grown-up' children is often overlooked or disbelieved. Older teenagers, perhaps those who are already at college or living away at university, spend few stretches of time at home and may seem only to make contact when they need something. Some parents accuse them of behaving like lodgers or of treating the home like a hotel. Do be careful, though, that you do not *treat* your daughter or son like a lodger or a guest. The home – particularly their room or space within it – and family members are acutely important to them as the safe base from which they came and to which they can return when outside life gets too difficult. That safe retreat is the emotional and geographical place from which they can launch themselves into adulthood. The fact that your child doesn't spend much time in the home or with you does not mean that either has become unimportant.

It isn't uncommon for parents to struggle or drift on in a more or less loveless marriage 'until the children leave home' and then split up. If you have stayed together 'for the sake of the children' you may have given them stability, as

Girl aged 18

Before I even left for uni, mum told me she was going to give my room to my sister so that she and my littlest sister had a room each and I could share with one of them when I came home. OK it sounds kind of reasonable, I know, but I really minded so much, especially when she packed all my stuff up. My dad knew I was upset and eventually he asked if I'd like to make the room I stayed in at his house into my own. It was nice of him but I couldn't really do that to my mum…

you intended, but you may also have presented them with a very chilly model of adult relationships. What's more the break-up, when it comes, may not be any easier for these nearly-adult children than it would have been years ago. If your teenager had thought – or assumed – that you were reasonably happy together (or hadn't given the matter any thought) and is now told that your separation has long been planned, he's liable to feel that if your relationship with each other was a lie so was his whole childhood and your relationships with him. A late family break-up may have less impact than an earlier one in the here-and-now but it has an enormous impact on the young person's sense of his own family history.

Boy aged 19

> *My parents stayed together for me until I'd done my GCSEs and started college. I didn't know that – no idea. When they told me they were splitting up and selling the house to buy a flat each they seemed to think I wouldn't care. No, worse than that: they seemed to think it was none of my business. I actually think that's why I made such a mess of everything.*

Young man aged 22

> *First I really couldn't believe what they were telling me. Truly. I had a moment there when I thought it must be a joke. But then it sank in and it just sort of stole my childhood. OK that sounds dramatic, but everything I'd known and trusted had been a lie and they'd been waiting for me to get out of the way so they could smash it up. I stayed angry for years. Actually I'm still angry. I'm not nearly as close to either of my parents as a lot of my friends are to theirs.*

Try not to assume that at 19 or even 20 your children are grown-up enough to be able to 'understand' why you have split up and be 'sensible' about it and 'fair' to both of you. Above all don't assume that because they have sexual relationships themselves they will sympathise with a parent's affair. Young people who are struggling to find themselves as adult men or women are often very judgemental about parents' behaviour and usually intensely embarrassed if they are forced to acknowledge their parents' sexuality. You are their mother and father not their friends. The less you confide in them the better.

Woman, looking back to when she was 14

> *When I was 14 my dad told me that one of the things he missed about my mother was her 'tip-tilted breasts'. Even as an adult and a parent myself I can't forgive his crass insensitivity. Talk about 'too much information'…*

3 Other people, inside & outside the family

Separation and divorce isn't nearly as private a matter as most couples think – or hope. Because our society and the care of the next generation are organised around marriage and monogamy, the break-up of a family touches many people directly. There are close relations and relations-by-marriage who may be deeply saddened for you both. Your own mother may wonder if she is partly responsible because she herself is divorced and brought you up without a father figure. In your own generation there may be brothers or sisters who are alarmed for themselves, feeling that if your apparently solid marriage has foundered their own may be at risk. A little further away there may be cousins and perhaps their girlfriends or boyfriends (and *their* families) who feel personally interested in what has happened and why. And then of course the break-up will be titillatingly interesting to almost every acquaintance who hears of it – and many will.

Not all these people will matter to your children, of course, but some will. Although parents are almost always the most important people in young children's lives and the most important adults all through adolescence, they are not the only ones. When parents separate having other people they are close to around – relatives or longstanding family friends – can make a tremendous difference both directly to the children themselves and indirectly because supported parents are more able to be supportive to their children.

3.1 Siblings

The most important people to a child, outside the bust-up trio of himself, his father and his mother, are usually siblings. During a parental break-up it is bad luck to be an 'only' child because children come through better if they have one or more brothers and sisters to share it with, whatever their ages and the age gaps between them and even if they haven't been especially close up to now. In middle childhood and in adolescence children may find it easier to talk about what is going on to each other than to anyone else. Where the age gap is too great for comfortable confidences, younger siblings can feel cared for and older siblings can feel caring. That often gives both children some of what they feel the breakdown of the family is taking from them: loving care.

Don't let yourself rely too much on the relationships between your children, though. You are the grown-ups. The fact that two teenagers support and confide in each other doesn't mean that they don't need to talk to you and your ex. And it is all too easy to let the care an older child gives to a younger one become burdensome for her.

Whatever their ages and however close they may feel, your children are not responsible for each other; you and their father are responsible for them and you may need to spell that out many times in addition to acting accordingly.

Above all, although you can count on simple companionship meaning that two or more children help each other to cope with this stressful time, don't assume, or let anyone, including the children themselves, assume that they feel exactly the same about the situation or aspects of it. One child may blame you for everything that's gone wrong while another blames her father. One may think his own bad behaviour was responsible for his dad leaving and another, enshrined as the family-good-kid, may thankfully agree because holding her brother responsible lets her off the hook. Later on one child may love going to father's house while another may find leaving you to spend time with him intolerable. Eventually one may like the new stepmother while another blames her for the break-up or resents her attempts at mothering.

You can't conjure up a sibling for your child, of course, any more than you can magically produce an extended family or support network. If there's only one child involved in your break-up the particular things you need to watch out for depend very much on her age (see Chapter 2). If she isn't yet school age she shouldn't be expected to be away from you overnight, though if she had a trusted older sibling he or she might help to keep separation anxiety in check. If she is a teenager or student, her companion and confidante would probably be a friend even if there was a sibling available. It's during the in-between years – say five to 14 – that being the only child of a broken family may be especially difficult. Whichever parent the child is with there are only the two of them and it is easy for them to come to depend on each other for company and support. There are girls not yet in their teens who feel that they ought to look after their lone fathers, domestically and even romantically, and boys who try to be the man of the house for their lone mothers. Sometimes well-

Girl aged 14

" When our parents finally split up I was 11 and Jack was eight and he really didn't like going to dad's flat on his own so we always went together. But now he's 11 he still always wants me to go too, and often I really need to be around with my friends. Dad understands that. He'd be cool with me meeting him for lunch sometimes instead of spending all day, but Jack really needs me. "

Girl aged 12

" Of course I knew he was lonely – he was so horribly pleased to see me at weekends that I couldn't ever say I wanted to stay at home for someone's birthday party. "

meaning but misguided relations and family friends actually exhort children to look after their parents. Unfortunately a lone father or mother is often also lonely and all too willing to step out of the parent role to make a companion, even confidante, of the child (see Chapter 5).

The more adult friends and supporters the parent has the more likely it is that he or she will be able to see adult life as continuing even without the partner, and the easier it will be for the child to see the parent as 'OK' and, hopefully, to relax and gradually relinquish the quasi-adult role. However, children in this situation can easily become jealous of anyone else their parent relies on, especially if it's a boyfriend or girlfriend.

Father of girl aged 14

I had come to rely a lot on my friend Maria. She quite often came round and cooked tea for us both at my place. She was dying to meet my daughter so she came on Saturday meaning to do a nice meal for the three of us but Rhianna would hardly speak to her. When she saw Maria in the kitchen cooking, she went mental and said I obviously didn't need her so she was going home. I asked my ex if it had been tactless of me to have Maria there and what she told me isn't repeatable!

Boy aged 11

She used to give me wine because she said she couldn't drink by herself. One day I told that to my dad and he was really really furious.

Boy aged 13

I know she's unhappy but I wish she wouldn't tell me why. I think it's what's called 'too much information'.

3.2 Grandparents

Grandparents are very special to a lot of children, and children are very special to a lot of grandparents. Many grandparents are special to their grandchildren's parents (their own adult children), too. In fact the popular assumption that grandchildren are even more beloved than children does not bear examination. Much of what grandparents do for their grandchildren they do to please their children and be involved in their lives.

The importance of grandparents to families in the Western world, especially to children, is seriously underestimated. Grandparents who live close by often provide the childcare that makes it possible for their daughter or daughter-in-law to work outside home. Grandparents who live too far away to provide hands-on help quite often help financially instead. A few help with the down-payment on a home. Some pay towards nursery costs or help out with extras such as school trips or music lessons for an older child.

Grandparents' contribution to children's care

Throughout the English-speaking world and starting from babyhood, more children who need care while parents are at work get it from grandparents than from anyone else.

Once they had any regular care from anyone but the mother, around a quarter of the American babies in the National Institute of Child Health and Human Development study and a similar proportion of the English babies in the Families, Children & Child care study were cared for by grandparents for an average of around thirty hours a week.

> " By the end of babies' first year, neither father care nor grandparent care is quite so predominant because other types of care are used more frequently. Grandparents continue to provide a large proportion of the total, however – often a larger proportion than is immediately obvious from statistical tables. When children are in more than one type of nonmaternal child care, the second or 'extra' type is usually grandparent care. In the FCCC study, for example, when children were in what was termed 'combination care' – family day care, say, plus something else – the something else was almost invariably care by a grandparent. And when grandparents' contribution to 'combined care' was added to the category of 'grandparent care,' it became clear that grandparents were providing more childcare than any other category of caregiver. "

Leach, 2010b

Even when grandparents are not their grandchildren's principal or secondary caregivers, and even if they undertake no regular childcare at all, many still make a large – if largely unrecorded and therefore hard to quantify – contribution to those children's care and wellbeing, including making an incalculable contribution to the parents' ability to hold down a job. Even if they do not undertake regular childcare, grandparents who live within easy reach of the grandchildren's home often serve as back-up caregivers who can be called upon to step in when regular arrangements go wrong. Even grandparents who live hours of travelling time away are sometimes called upon to come and stay with children who are too ill for their regular childcare, so that parents need not take time off from work.

By no means all grandparents welcome these commitments. They want to see and spend time with their children and grandchildren but would rather do so socially and when it suited them. Many speak sadly of having had to abandon plans for leisure and travel in retirement. In a recent Australian study, some grandparents expressed open resentment at any assumption that they would take on the role of childcare provider for their grandchildren and objected to this role being expected of them by their children or the community.

Maternal grandmother of three children

> " If I could say no without turning my daughter's work life upside down, and without losing my chance to see the children and her regularly, I would. "

However, a grandparent who stands in for or backs up parents in caring for a child while the family is intact, especially if they have done so from babyhood, is likely to be highly placed in that child's 'attachment hierarchy'. Mother will come first and probably father next, but the third most important person in his life may well be a grandmother (or perhaps a grandfather) who will therefore be in an ideal position to help if the family breaks up.

Many grandfathers have moved into new roles with children just as their sons and sons-in-law have done. Many are, and are expected to be, interested in their grandchildren as well as loving, and their presence in the lives of father-deprived children can be invaluable. One grandfather, newly retired, expressed the sentiments of many when he said, 'When my children were growing up, I was so busy making a living I had very little time for them. Now my biggest joy is being with my grandchildren. Maybe I'm trying to make up for what I didn't do before.' Although grandfathers, especially maternal grandfathers who have retired from work, often spend a lot of time with their grandchildren, even taking part in grandparent childcare, they almost always do it in partnership with their wives. Very few grandfathers take sole or even main responsibility for the care of a grandchild, whether he or she is being looked after at home or taken out for a treat.

Grandfathers caring for grandchildren

When grandfathers reported looking after grandchildren, only 4% of those interviewed said they took the main responsibility of care, while around half shared it with their partner or spouse and nearly half said their partner or spouse was solely responsible for the grandchildren. In contrast, more than half (54%) of the grandmothers reported taking the main responsibility of care for grandchildren, with just over one-third saying they shared the responsibility with their partner or spouse.

Millward, 1998

Grandparents are not important only to babies and toddlers. A large survey of childcare in the UK published in 2006 showed that almost one in five (19%) of all families using childcare and/or early years education for a preschool child (up to age five) relied principally on care by a grandparent.

And grandparent care does not necessarily end even when children reach school age. In Australia in 2002, more children under the age of 12 received informal care by a grandparent than any other kind of care, formal or informal, while in 2006 The British Daycare Trust stated that each week a quarter of families with children under 15 used a grandparent to look after a child for an average of 16 hours per week, and many adolescents, who don't exactly need care and probably wouldn't be offered it from any other source, welcome grandparents' caring companionship when parents are not around.

Boy aged 13

" In the holidays Gran and Gramps always say 'pop round if you need anything' and I do go round quite a lot. It's not exactly that I need anything – though Gran's a stellar cook – it's that hanging out with them makes a change from hanging out with my mates. "

The particular importance of grandparents to teenage grandchildren is highlighted in a study of communication in British families. During the survey period, more than one in five of the teenagers who had spent time with a grandparent while their parents were at work had talked to that grandparent about personal issues and problems, including family breakdown, a higher proportion than had discussed such things with parents, teachers or siblings.

Given the overwhelming importance of grandparents to many contemporary families, it is astonishing how little factual information we have about them. Even their identity is surrounded by question marks. It might seem that biology makes it perfectly clear who is and is not whose grandparent, but does it? If your child's grandmother is your husband's mother, she's your mother-in-law; if she's your mother, she's his mother-in-law, but what if she is his or your stepmother? One thing we do know is that not all grandparents are loved and loving, and if yours are not it is very likely due to family breakdown in an earlier generation.

Two generations of divorce

> *Poor relationships between today's parents and grandparents are often planted in yesterday's anxieties and misunderstandings, predating the birth of the first grandchild. A divorce puts 'ex' in front of most relationship names, and a remarriage introduces 'step'. Is the father of a parent's live-in lover her children's grandfather? And what about the new partner of the grandfather himself? Is she – or he – your children's step-grandmother or step-grandfather even if the role has not been formalised by law and the original partner is still around?*

Leach, 2010b

What we also know is that although research studies involving extended families do not always clearly distinguish between grandparents and other relatives, between maternal and paternal grandparents or even between grandmothers and grandfathers, and while there are certainly aunts, cousins and step-everybodies who are lastingly important to children when immediate families break-up, the relatives who are likely to matter most, in every country, are maternal grandmothers: mothers' biological or adoptive mothers and very occasionally stepmothers.

Unfortunately parental separation does not always bring grandparents closer to their children and grandchildren. Sometimes that special relationship shrivels in the cold blast of family breakdown, with less and less contact between grandparents and grandchildren, not only while a separation or divorce is underway but forever afterwards. Since it is the maternal grandmother, often supported by the maternal grandfather, who is most likely to be closely involved in supporting the separated family, and her support will be going to the mother and children, paternal grandparents are very vulnerable to gradual exclusion and fathers are likely to be left without much support from their own parents. In research surveys parents mostly say that it is important for children to have as much contact with both sets of grandparents after their parents are separated or divorced as they did before, but in real life that doesn't often happen. Many parents cannot help seeing the two older generation households as enemy camps and cannot tolerate the idea of older children confiding private details of one parent's life to the parents of the other.

Currently in the UK grandparents have no legal rights to see their grandchildren but if the parents should forbid this, grandparents can apply to the court for permission to apply for a contact order (see Chapter 4.5). In the meantime various organisations are campaigning for grandparents' rights and some, especially in the United States, are successfully having them recognised. Such measures may help grandparents but do not seem likely to help the grandchildren.

Children can gain immeasurable support from grandparents who are closely and warmly involved with their separating parents as well as with them, but they are unlikely to find it helpful to have yet another adult fighting one or both parents for contact with them.

Mother of toddler aged 18 months

" *I know they love him. And he loves them too. But taking him to see them is really hard for me because they've never really liked me, not from the first time their son took me to a movie. They didn't think I was good enough for him then and now they're sure I'm not.* "

Grandparents in separated families

The Grandparents in Separated Families Study featured focus groups with 50 grandparents discussing their experience 'of the effects of parental separation on relationships with their grandchildren, their adult children and their adult children's former partners. The findings provide insight into the causes and consequences of such issues as relocation and geographical distance, financial capacity, family relationships, moral judgements of right and wrong, commitment, use of legal processes, and fairness, all of which appear to contribute to the growth or decline of post-separation relationships for grandparents.'

Deblaquiere, Moloney and Weston, 2012

3.3 Extended family & other special adults

When parents are behaving oddly, it helps children of all ages to have other adults around whom they know and trust and who are still behaving normally. Different adults may be special to different children: one may hang on to a grandparent or caregiver; another may spend more and more time with the family of his best friend who lives close by, while it may be a teacher at school or college who is the most vital support for an older child or young adult.

Having your child strike up a close and confidential relationship with another adult – especially if it is not a family member – can leave you feeling hurt and anxious. Your child stays late after school several days a week or spends more and more time in another home and gradually it becomes clear that it's not just to spend time with a friend but also to spend time with one or other of the teachers or parents. Why will your child talk to that adult when he absolutely refuses to talk to you? Why will she take their advice and accept their comfort when she shrugs off yours? Try to understand that those adults are more acceptable and useful to your child right now just because they are not you. With the family collapsing around her she is no longer sure what your values, judgements and viewpoints are, or whether she can go on assuming that what you do and say represents the adult world. She needs to find out whether other adults, especially adults she has sought out for herself, think and behave differently from you.

Such relationships with other parents, with teachers or any other caring adults, can be truly valuable to an adolescent. If you do find yourself enviously resenting them, remind yourself that the child is trying to understand what is happening in her family and her own feelings about it and that if she cannot get sufficient help from family members she is better off getting it from outside the family than not getting it at all. However, children who are unhappy and confused by what is going on at home are especially vulnerable to relationships with outsiders that cross the line from appropriate to inappropriate concern. If there is such an adult in your child's life and you find yourself anxious about the relationship, it will be both helpful to your child and protective of her if both of you parents agree to share at least an outline of what is going on with the child's chosen adult so that she knows it's all right for her to confide if she wants to (see Chapter 5.1). Do remember, though, that such an adult confidante is no more likely to treat your child irresponsibly than you would be if you were similarly placed with somebody else's child. One day perhaps you will be.

Most people that either of you tell about trouble in your family will inevitably take sides, of course. But if the two of you together confide in someone who is truly concerned for you all as a family, is especially concerned for the children and does you both the honour of assuming that they are your main concern too, he or she may provide you all with emotional ballast during the stormiest times. Be careful who you pick, though. Some people will make an enjoyable drama out of the sadness you are recounting, and enjoy passing it on, too. And an obtuse or insensitive adult can rip scabs off children instead of putting sticking plaster on.

It's not only your children who need support: as you and your partner tear yourselves apart you are both going to need other adults you can rely on. In theory every nuclear family is the nucleus of an extended family. In practise, though, in our individualistic society, a nuclear family is often a more-or-less stand-alone unit consisting only of a couple in a sexual partnership and children for whom they are solely responsible. That kind of family isn't the nucleus of anything, so instead of having support networks you can take for granted, you may have to work for them. Grandparents are an obvious starting point but sadly, although many parents rely on grandparents for childcare or babysitting if they happen to live nearby, as we have seen, not many intact couples regard the relationship between themselves and their own parents, or between grandparents and grandchildren, as highly important to family life. Few, for example, will turn down a change of job, or even of country, because it will take them much further away.

If you are separating you might regret having taken a cavalier approach to available grandparents – and even rethink it as you face up to the next stages of your family's life. Nuclear families are all very well as long as all's well, but if there is nothing and nobody to support them from outside they are horribly vulnerable to disintegration if that central couple-relationship goes wrong. It is when that is happening that the importance of extended family – or any other kind of support from outside – becomes painfully clear.

Woman, now aged 50

" I was 12 and at boarding school, desperately miserable about what was going on at home, especially the brand new stepmother who'd arrived in dad's house. The school matron caught me crying and I confided this to her. Do you know what she said? She said 'you're really lucky to have two mothers'. "

Man, now aged 30

" My mum's stepmother was really shocked when my mother left my father and moved in with another guy, a bit younger than her. I was about ten and I'd been told that they planned to marry and that my sisters and I could go and live with them. 'He may marry Emily,' said my grandmother, 'but there's no way he's going to take on you lot… Why would he?' "

Father of three daughters aged 2, 6 and 8 years

> *Her mum, dad, two aunts and an uncle lived three doors down from us. I'd sometimes felt they were a bit too much in our faces, if you know what I mean, but when I moved out and moved away I realised just how important they were, and to me as well as to her.*
>
> *Her dad and her uncle were the people I went to the pub with. That held me together during the worst months before we separated, and not having that was one of the loneliest bits of living on my own. To my ex and the kids their house was an extension of ours. I think it was the popping in and out that held her together, plus any or all of the women took care of Mandy so she had time to herself. Without it, she says, Mandy would have had a pretty boring six months and seen and heard a lot of crying and screaming. Kate liked to go and join in after school. She specially loved one of the aunties who had lots of laughs for her at a time when her mum really didn't. And Jenny: well, being a bit older, I suppose, she worried about her mum and about me and about what was going to happen, and she took all that to her gran...*

You obviously cannot invent loving relatives or even form friendship networks in the time it takes your marriage to break down, but do be aware of the importance of any you already have when you make decisions about separating and who is going to live where. One of you is going to be a lone parent and the other is going to be a mostly lone *person*. And for each of you lone will often mean lonely. The kind of support you need may be mostly emotional, mostly practical or both. People who love you and will always be there for you are a huge emotional resource wherever they live, even Australia if you all use video chat. But people don't have to live halfway across the world to be too far away to be useful on a day-to-day basis.

Next-door neighbours, whose children feel like your kids' cousins, may be such an important asset (hopefully to both families) that they are something to take into account when you're thinking about selling and moving. If you must move house and can't stay with the same neighbours, think about staying in the same neighbourhood so that the children can at least stay at the same schools with friends and familiar teachers, and you don't lose the friends you have made at the school gate. School gate support networks *are* a big part of daily life, especially while you have a child at pre- or primary school, but you may not want all of them to know too much about your private affairs – which they will if you tell any of them. If you must move right out of the district to a new community, could you make a virtue out of the necessity by moving close to the grandparents you've never been able to see enough of, or even close to those old friends who moved away last year?

3.4 Parents' lovers & potential partners

Parents separate for 'grown-up' reasons and often because one or both of them want a new and different 'grown-up' life. Sometimes those reasons are clear fault lines in the original marriage, such as one or both partners being abusive, alcoholic or perhaps addicted to drugs or gambling. But often those 'grown-up' reasons are to do with having found, or being on the lookout for, a new sexual partnership and when that's the case it's especially difficult to put children first.

If your marriage is falling apart primarily over an affair with another man or woman, children will soon know and if they are old enough to think about other people's relationships at all – over seven, say – will probably see the stranger as having straightforwardly stolen one parent from the other. There is a childish parallel in shifting best friendships at school and children may find such a 'theft' a more comprehensible – and even forgivable – reason for parents separating than the incomprehensible emotional betrayal of just not loving each other anymore. But if children usually forgive the 'stolen' parent-as-victim, they may not easily forgive the person who 'stole' him or her. If the love affair turns out to be a life affair this can be a nightmarish route into step-parenting.

If another person comes on your scene after you have separated and new living arrangements have been achieved, do your ex the courtesy of telling him or her before anyone else does. Don't be in a hurry to tell your children, though, or to introduce him or her to them. They may deeply resent anyone who even looks like edging into a missing parent's place, but that's the less dire of two equally probable possibilities. Children who have recently lost their taken-for-granted-everyday father are often easily enraptured by the making-an-effort charms of a new candidate. If he plays football in the garden with the middle one, shoulders the littlest one on walks, talks usefully to the oldest about her forthcoming exam and makes you laugh, he may soon be a welcome visitor and within weeks an important part of the children's life. If the two of you then decide that the relationship is not going anywhere – and face it, not many affairs do – childish hearts will be broken all over again. Not because losing this lover-man is as bad as losing their dad, but because losing their dad has left them acutely vulnerable to loss and the household short of an adult male. Although children react differently to changes to a household they visit rather than live in, roughly the same possibilities apply if the children's father introduces a new lover.

Research specifically on this point is rather sparse but what there is strongly suggests that it's best to keep the new person merely as one of your friends in the children's eyes, holding back any sense of the relationship being special and any business of theirs until you are truly convinced that it is going to be long-lasting and a partnership is planned between you and ready for implementation.

Until that time comes (if it ever does):

- Don't have a new sexual partner staying overnight with you when the children are in the house. Their reaction to finding you in bed or in the shower together will vary according to their ages but every variation will be disastrous.
- Don't underestimate children's ability to pick up clues to this 'friendship' being special. It doesn't take finding an intimate garment in the laundry basket to raise a child's suspicions; switching to the brand of tea he or she prefers or changing the newspaper you take may be enough.
- If the children live with you don't encourage – or even allow – a new lover the privilege of parent-like behaviour with your children, however tempting it may be to enlist his or her skills in making a birthday cake, picking up your daughter from a late party or backing up your discipline.
- If the children live with your ex, don't try to squeeze in extra time with your lover by joining him or her into the time you spend with your children. When they come to visit, they want to see you and only you and they want to see you as you are with them not as you are with your new partner.
- Try not to change access arrangements simply in order to give yourself more child-free time to spend with this new person. If a month ago you didn't think it was a good idea for your two-year-old to sleep over with her father at weekends, it is almost certainly not a good idea now.

If and when you are seriously contemplating making this relationship a partnership:

- If you want to try out the business of living together as a potential family group, try and do it on neutral territory rather than by inviting him or her to come and live with you and the children. If the money and the time can be afforded, a rented holiday home is often a good start. Nobody's territory is being invaded; nobody knows how to manage this environment so everyone can work out the ground rules for living in it together.

- Make sure your potential new partner realises that your children already have two parents (even if they only see one at a time) and don't need any more. Sometimes well-meaning people assume that lone parents want help with their parenting when what they really want help with is the lone bit. Make it clear that if all goes well, he or she can eventually become a highly significant adult in your children's lives but never their parent.
- Beware of authority. Few children will readily accept instructions or reproofs from a comparative stranger, but many adults find it difficult to *live with* children without giving any. If your potential partner cannot manage this now, it is very likely to become a problem if you eventually marry.
- Beware of manipulation. Many children work hard to influence parents' choice of partner, usually in the direction of getting rid of them. Techniques vary from the blatant (spiders in shoes) to the more subtle (pretend she isn't there at all). Either can be most successfully off-putting.
- Be sure it is understood that whatever the issue, you are and must be a parent first before you are a partner, and that as a parent you will be communicating with your ex and doing your best to maintain a co-operative mutual – or at least polite – relationship.

3.5 Children's step-parents

Even if your child has known the soon-to-be step-parent for many months and really likes him or her, you may find that once he knows you plan an actual marriage his attitude changes for the worse. Perhaps the often extreme difficulties step-parents may have in relating to younger children start with ideas about step-parents that children draw from fairy stories, in which both sexes are invariably wicked and cruel. As for older children and teenagers, they may have replaced fairy-tale stereotypes about step-parents with awareness of the bad press given to step-parents, especially stepfathers, as perpetrators of child abuse.

Children can develop extremely close and warm relationships with step-parents. Some even maintain that, despite the misery at the time, they are glad there was a divorce:

Girl, now aged 16

> *I was 12 when they finally decided they wanted to get married and I realised I was going to have a stepfather. I don't know what got into me but I told a pack of made up lies about him to my school friends – stupid things like he wore sandals with socks which he never did – and to my Gran. I even told Gran I didn't want to live with him and could I come and live with her. It's lucky I didn't make things up and tell them to my dad or it might really have caused trouble. But why did I tell my best friend I hated him? I liked him a lot and I'd known him for nearly two years as our closest family friend…*

Boy aged 12

> *I'm closer to my stepdad than I've ever been or ever would have been to my real father. I just like him better. I think he's a much nicer man. And he makes my mum laugh. As to my littlest sister, she's three now and I think she really feels like he's daddy. She doesn't call him daddy 'cause mum says things like 'you've got one of those already' but she calls him 'my-Da' in a soppy sort of a voice. Mum thought I might mind but I don't.*

Most children whose parents have divorced are not at all glad to have a step-parent, though. Many have found it impossible to accept that their parents' separation is permanent and though the divorce has been finalised they often go on for years dreaming of a reconciliation. Even for a child who really knows that a dream is only a dream and isn't going to happen, the idea of a parent marrying for a second time and finally moving those dream goalposts from improbable to impossible is difficult to cope with.

Helping your children to accept the prospect and reality of a step-parent

- Although children survive the trauma of parental separation better if other aspects of life can stay the same (see Chapter 4), the positive step of making a new family grouping usually works more easily in a new environment. In these circumstances a house move often makes a better start than having all of you move in with him (or her) or vice versa. In a new home, everyone shares mutual territory about which nobody feels possessive, and there can be mutual ground rules for living in it from the beginning.

- Leaving room for the 'real' parent is vital. That means room in the child's life – so that his regular visiting days and weekends don't suddenly get lost in new-family activities – and psychological room, too. Don't expect him to call the step-parent 'mum' or 'dad', for example (unless he asks, or does it spontaneously), or push him to make Mother's Day cards for the stepmother instead of, or even as well as, his real mother.

- Try to make the new relationship completely extra to rather than instead-of the original one. And make sure room is left for the old family, too. Encourage children's relationships with your ex's family and don't expect them to drop old family stories, in-jokes and so forth. Tell them to the new person instead.

- Although their relationship is *because* of you, the step-parent and children cannot make it *through* you. Try not to stand in the middle, like a maypole around which everybody dances. The step-parent and children have to get to know one another as people rather than as your appendages. However jealous a child may seem to be of the newcomer, she will notice your new happiness and give him or her credit for it; eventually she will probably be ready to seek a share for herself.

- Don't expect the step-parent *or* children to accept sex-stereotyped family roles too quickly (if at all). A stepfather, for example, usually needs to go very easily on 'discipline', 'manners' and so forth. With adolescents he may never be permitted an authoritative relationship but may, if he will accept it, eventually be offered friendship instead. A stepmother will probably need to hold back on personal care, however warmly she feels towards the children. She is likely to be felt to be 'stepping beyond the bounds' if she tries to plait hair or wash necks, at least until the children spontaneously hug and kiss her.

- Try to arrange for the step- and natural parent to meet, especially if you have managed to keep your relationship with your ex civil since the divorce. Children need to feel that all the adults who are closely concerned with them are on the same side – their side. It also helps if they do not feel that they can at all easily play one off against the other or have their wilder fantasies believed.

4 Practical & legal issues

A baby or toddler's environment and lifestyle is dominated by his relationships with the people he is attached to – principally mother and then father. But as he grows through toddlerhood and into a preschool child and then a schoolchild, parents remain central but other things come to matter too. As you struggle with the sadness and the guilt of parental separation, you may find it comforting and helpful to realise what a lot of practical aspects of your children's changing lives you can control, and how much that can do to protect or rebuild their happiness and wellbeing.

The change from having both parents living with them in the same home to having the two of you living in separate places is one of the biggest a child can ever meet. It is not just a storm but a hurricane that howls through family life, rocking all the relationships and wrecking children's security. You cannot avoid that change (if it were possible for you to stay together no doubt you would be doing so) but parental separation tends to bring other changes along with it and some of these you may be able to avoid. If you can, you should. Moving to a new home, changing from one caregiver or nursery to another or going to a new school are all normal life-events, that are highly stressful to most children even if they are securely embedded in intact families. But when normal events such as these are part of the abnormal disruption of the family caused by parental separation, they can be not just stressful but devastating. When family is in turmoil the more smoothly the rest of their lives can carry on as before, the better children will cope. So before you plan on – or just accept – big changes like the ones dealt with in this chapter, make sure you ask yourselves – and each other – about other options. Above all, think geography.

4.1 Family geography & children's security

Children's security depends on the people to whom they are attached being available. When parents separate children lose the security of being able to take the presence of both of them together or either one of them at a time for granted. That's a huge loss but just how acute and lasting it is largely depends on everybody's proximity. Daddy has left and that's awful, but where has he gone? The answer 'into a flat in the next road' is less awful than 'the other side of town' and very, *very* much less awful than 'a three-hour journey away', not to mention 'to Australia' or, worst of all, 'I don't know'. Although everything that is most important and most difficult about making a separated family work for children depends primarily on parents maintaining a reasonable relationship with each other, staying within easy geographical reach comes a close second.

Avoiding the other big, stressful changes in your children's lifestyle that will make parental separation harder to bear is also largely a matter of geography. If after daddy leaves you could find a way of staying in the same home, the children could keep the bedrooms and the play space they are used to; keep the family cat or the beloved rabbits; stay in the same schools and keep their whole network of friends and neighbours, and so could you. Even if staying in the same house is financially impossible, they could still keep the familiar infrastructure of their lives if you could find the smaller, cheaper home you need in the same neighbourhood.

4.2 The need for a home base

However many places there are where he spends time, a child must live somewhere, must have a home. A place and setting that we think of as 'home' is highly important to most of us but it may be especially so to children because they have so little control over their own lives and lack adults' nest-making experience and skills. If you move, temporarily or permanently, you will know where you are going – even if you go reluctantly – and whether it is into a new flat, a hotel room or a prison cell, you will at once settle down to making the new place feel as homelike as you can. A child who is moved has no idea where he is going or what it will be like. If the new place is stable and somebody helps him settle in it he will eventually get past the fact that it is not home so that it can become so and give him back his security. But until or unless he has a home base his life will lack stability.

Almost all children do move house; on average families in the UK and the USA move four to six times while children are growing up. But most house moves are job-related, are chosen (or at least accepted) by the parents and maintain or even upgrade the family's standard of living. A house move resulting from a family break-up is different; it is not something that both parents have chosen, indeed the loss of one parent is implicit in it, and as if that huge change in the family's lifestyle was not painful enough the new place will usually be a step down. The contrast experienced by the 11-year-old quoted below when she was moved from isolated countryside to inner-city living was extreme, but her devastation is nevertheless noteworthy because if her parents had been more aware of the issues that were critical to her they might have managed a less lastingly traumatic move.

Woman, looking back to when she was 11

> *It wasn't just moving house it was moving life. We'd lived deep in the country ever since I could remember (actually since I was three). I'd had a pony since I was seven. She was the centre of everything I did and most of what I thought, too. Leaving her behind just felt like everything had come to an end. Like I had come to an end. And I didn't understand how to be in London. How could you play in a little garden with people either side and rows of windows looking at you? Was I angry with them? No. I was too sad, too bewildered to be angry. I think I was grown-up and a parent myself before I could feel properly furious.*

Do arrange for the children and whichever parent is to live with them to stay in their existing home if that is at all possible, at least during the upheaval of the actual separation. They will get used to a home with only one parent in it a great deal more easily if the home *is* home. Changes within that home will probably be less disturbing than a move. A (carefully selected) lodger, for example, might bring a mortgage within reach without bothering children nearly as much as leaving the house. Be careful about doubling the children up so as to free a bedroom to rent out, though. Once children have had a bedroom each those separate rooms often become exceedingly important – perhaps especially to teenagers – and being suddenly forced to share can jeopardise sibling relationships just when they are at their most important.

before. If after-school sports are mostly on Fridays, a tired, dirty child and all his gear will arrive late for the start of your precious weekend.

Don't feel that you have to try and make both places as like each other as possible. A four- or five-year-old may settle more easily if his bedding is familiar and the nightlight is 'right', but as long as even slightly older children feel secure in the place they think of as 'home' and are able to leave it and the resident parent easily, the fact that the other parent's place is different can be part of the pleasure of regular visits, in addition to the pleasure of spending time with him. Differences between the two homes can be part of the fun, giving children a bit of space in which to be different people. Different food, different music, different conversation, different games and different ground rules can all be interesting extensions of life at home.

4.3 Schools

Sometimes parents forget how important school is to a child. While the routines of going to school, the school's hours, the breaks and the holiday dates are an important part of the structure of family life, and will lend children stability during the upheavals of parental separation, what actually goes on in school can strike parents as a mixture of mystery and trivia and something they don't have to think much about. Parents who are very taken up with other things such as problems between them and trying to work out how to manage a separation are especially likely to take school for granted and think about the home-child they see and know as if that was the whole child. It is not the whole child, of course. That same home-child actually has to live those unseen hours, becoming a schoolchild for the whole of every day the school is open and with no choice in the matter unless he convinces you that he is ill.

Folk-wisdom says that 'school days are the happiest days of your life'. It's sad to think of a whole adult life offering no greater happiness than being a schoolchild, but if school days are not at least moderately and mostly happy, your child will be unhappy overall. He has got to spend most of the waking hours of around 245 days of each year in school. It is not just a place where he goes to learn while his 'real life' carries on at home. It is the place where he will have (or not have) most of his friends; where he will make (or not make) most of his meaningful relationships with non-family adults; where he will find (or fail to find) most of his sporting and leisure activities. School will, and should be, central to his life, so no parent is entitled to ignore what goes on there.

Getting support from school

School may be especially important to children when parents are separating, because when things are in a muddle at home, school can provide much-needed structure and predictability, and being with peers may be a welcome distraction. If your very young child is liable to be tearful and visibly upset at school, it may be helpful to tell her teacher what is going on at home – or at least that something is – so that she can keep a sympathetic eye on her. An older child may not want anyone to know about your separation and you should respect his or her confidence if you can. But if teachers express surprise because a previously co-operative student is being difficult, even aggressive, it is obviously better that they should know that he is under particular stresses so that any complaints about his behaviour are dealt with as sympathetically as possible.

Sometimes it is not your child's behaviour at school that causes anxiety but difficulty in getting him to school. Acute anxiety over going to school may be triggered by something that happened to you, not to him, and made him wonder if you were 'all right'. Sometimes the trigger is an obviously traumatic one, such as parents actually separating, but sometimes it is something more trivial. A minor depression, perhaps, which made the child aware that you were unhappy, or an overheard row between you and his father, which made him wonder whether all was well between you or whether his family was going to break-up.

Once a child is sensitive to your welfare and feels that he has to keep an eye out to be sure you are 'all right', being away at school all day can become intolerable because he imagines all the fearful things that may have happened to you while he was gone. Will you be there when he gets home? Will he find you crumpled in a pool of blood or in floods of tears? Will you have 'gone mad' so that you no longer know or love him? Once his imagination runs riot in this way, logical probabilities and possibilities cannot comfort him. The level of his anxiety will probably vary from day to day. At its worst, the anxiety may show up in physical symptoms such as stomach pains, that make it impossible for him eat breakfast, or headaches or migraines. When his anxiety level is very high some or all of his typical physical symptoms may show up not only when he is actually faced with going to school, but also when he is made to think about, or discuss, going to school.

That fear and fear-of-fear make a vicious circle. The child who finds himself 'in a state' on Monday mornings soon comes to dread those horrible feelings as well as the school which first evoked them (see Chapter 8.1).

Do go immediately to see whichever teacher is concerned
with your child's wellbeing and enlist the school's help for him.
Meanwhile, make sure that the child understands what is going
on between you and his father, what is going to happen and
what you feel about it. The reality is sad but it is nowhere near as
terrifying as those fantasies. Between your efforts and those of a
sympathetic teacher he may be able to cope, but if someone else
to talk to would make it easier you can probably enlist further
help from the school psychological service.

Changing schools

Going to a new school is a big and important change for most
children. Regular moves as children get older are built in to the
school systems of different countries, with the big UK moves being
into school 'reception' at four or five, from primary to secondary
school at 11+ and from secondary school to sixth form or college
at 16+. The equivalents in the US are starting kindergarten, then
moving into elementary school, then middle school or junior
high, then high school, college or university. Those regular moves
are recognised as stressful for children, not only because new
institutions with their different organisational structures and
demands are always daunting, but also because leaving the
school a child is settled in always involves losing some important
relationships which have to be replaced in the new one.

Children who move at the expected 'transition' times and within
the same community will usually find themselves moving up
the system with at least some classmates and into a school
that knows where they have come from and has probably put
a lot of thought into its 'transition arrangements'. The children
who are likely to find the move really difficult are the ones who
move from one school to another outside those expected times,
especially if they move mid-year and perhaps to a different part
of the country. If your child is mid-way through primary school or
part-way through secondary school, you obviously cannot wait
to move him until he reaches the next conventional moving age.
But whatever age he is you may be able to avoid moving him
mid-year just by prevaricating on your house sale or purchase. If
you find the idea of 'going slow' acceptable and it is unlikely to
pose a risk to the final deal, it may be worth doing.

Part of the importance of the relationships children make in
school and the activities they take up is that they are separate
from you and from home. You cannot do it for him (as you may
have done in nursery or preschool), but you may be able to
help him do it for himself. Whatever the age of the child there
is always a fine line to be drawn between interference and

neglect in a parent's dealings with a school. The happy medium has something to do with always being interested enough to listen, and a lot to do with always being willing, even eager, to be involved whenever the child or the school issues any kind of invitation. When your child is starting at a school where he knows nobody and is the only one who is new, a bit of extra parental participation will certainly help, but what will help most of all is your awareness of what he is up against and your ability to sense when he is struggling and wants your support, and when he is managing himself and wants to live his school life without any parental involvement at all.

As well as being immediately stressful for children, extra and ill-timed school moves may also reduce school performance.

Between the cracks

Figures from the Royal Society of Arts Education think-tank show that children who change schools outside the traditional first years of primary and secondary education in England do worse in exams than peers who do not; the decline in attainment increases with each change of school.

300,000 children move schools each year. Children from families eligible for free school meals – with a household income of less than £25,000 a year – make up about 40% of the total, well above the 26% of pupils who receive free meals nationally.

However, poverty and disadvantage does not fully explain the ill effects of these school moves:

'Even after adjusting for prior attainment and social background, we're confident that there is a negative impact happening to these people because of in-year moves.'

Report from the Royal Society of Arts Education think-tank, 2013

Apart from stress-related problems, including anxiety over leaving home (see above), there seem to be two main reasons why children's education suffers from moving school between years other than the conventional ones, or in mid-year. Firstly, these children are often moved from one school to another because their families can no longer afford to continue living where they are. When a family moves to a less expensive area, or seeks cheaper accommodation some distance away, the children are likely to be admitted to lower-performing schools because these are the only schools that have unfilled places. Secondly, moving schools may mean missing substantial chunks of schooling. In many parts of the UK it is not easy to find a child a mid-year place in any new school, even a lower-performing one. Figures from the national pupil database show that in any one year there will be 20,000 pupils who are still without a place in a new school a whole term after leaving the old one.

So, however hard you try to work with the system, and however flexible you are prepared to be about the distance your child travels from a new home to a new school, that child may find himself without any school place for many weeks and then in a school that you would never have chosen for him. If his schoolwork was already suffering in reaction to the family breakdown (see Chapters 2.3, 2.4 and 2.5) what should have been a temporary dip in his educational attainment may become a lasting drop.

4.4 Money matters

Parents' ability to keep the practical aspects of family life running smoothly while the emotional part is struggling unfortunately depends largely on money.

Don't underestimate the costs of getting a divorce in the first place. In the UK a reasonably co-operative divorce will cost around £1,300, which is about 3% of the annual salary of a well-to-do family and as much as 9% of the least well-paid. In the United States costs vary from state to state but average out at around $15,000. If the two of you cannot work out the terms of your divorce between you so that solicitors have to be enlisted, the costs of your divorce will soar and so will its emotional costs to your children. The more you fight the more they will suffer.

As we have seen (see Introduction), people who are well-off are less likely to get divorced in the first place, but if they do split up a good income certainly helps to dress everybody's wounds. However comfortably well off you may be when your separation becomes inevitable, though, it is likely that you will be very much poorer by the time things settle down.

- The resources that have supported one home and family will have to support two.
- Some expensive possessions may have to be doubled up – the car for instance.
- Resources may dwindle if, for example, it is impossible for both of you to go on working full-time because childcare arrangements that formerly made it possible (such as a nanny or a full-time nursery place) are no longer affordable.

- If you and the children move out of the neighbourhood, childcare help that was available without cost from grandparents or friends may be out of geographical reach.
- If the other parent moves out of the district, staying in contact with the children will depend on there being money for travel.

Single-parent families & poverty in the UK, 2013

- Children in single parent families have a much higher risk of living in poverty than children in couple families. Around four in every ten (41%) children in single parent families are poor, compared to just over two in every ten children in couple families.
- Paid work is not a guaranteed route out of poverty for single parents; the poverty rate for single parent families where the parent works part-time is 23%; where the parent works full-time it is 18%.
- The median weekly income of working single parent families doing 16 hours a week or more is £337, compared with £491 for couple families with one worker and £700 where both parents work.
- Single parent households are the most likely to be in arrears on one or more household bills, mortgage or non-mortgage borrowing commitment (31%).
- 32% of working single parents who are paying for childcare, as compared with 22% of couples where one partner is in work, find it difficult to meet those costs. 34% had a childcare arrangement with the child's grandparent; 17% had an arrangement with their ex-partner.
- 43% of single parents are social housing tenants compared to 12% of couples.
- 71% of all single parent renters were eligible for UK housing benefit in 2011 compared to 25% of all couple renters.
- 38% of single parents said that money always runs out before the end of the week/month compared to 19% of couples.
- 63% of single parents have no savings compared to 34% of couples.

The Facts About Single Parents, Gingerbread.org.uk, 2013

Child maintenance

Child maintenance is the term used for financial support that helps towards a child's everyday living costs. Child maintenance is for children under 16 (or under 20 for children in full-time education). It is paid by the parent who doesn't have day-to-day care of the child (the 'paying parent') to the parent or person such as a grandparent or guardian who does (the 'receiving parent'). There are statutory services on both sides of the Atlantic (the Child Support Agency, or CSA, and the Child Maintenance Service in the UK; the Office of Child Support in the USA) which will work out how much ought to be paid in your particular circumstances and will, in theory at least, collect it for you.

Service in the USA is provided by, and varies between, states. In the UK changes were made in the child support system in 2012 to encourage more couples to make their own arrangements. Many of those who continue to seek help from the statutory bodies will have to pay towards the service.

Help is available from statutory child maintenance services (UK & USA)

These services can help you to:

- Sort out any issues concerning parentage, arranging DNA testing if necessary (www.gov.uk/arranging-child-maintenance-child-support-agency/disagreements-about-parentage).
- Work out how much child maintenance should be paid (www.gov.uk/how-child-maintenance-is-worked-out).
- Look at the payments again when either parent reports changes in their circumstances (www.gov.uk/arranging-child-maintenance-child-support-agency/changes-you-need-to-report).
- Take action if payments are not made, including having the employer withhold money from the paying parent's pay packet or benefits (www.gov.uk/arranging-child-maintenance-child-support-agency/nonpayment-what-happens; www.acf.hhs.gov/programs/css).
- Find the other parent if you do not have an address
- Arrange for the 'paying parent' to pay child maintenance.
- Pass payments on to the 'receiving parent'.

Unfortunately these services are not always as good as they sound. Don't overestimate this source of financial help with caring for your children after you have separated from their other parent. The system is overburdened and unwieldy so despite the large range and draconian nature of the measures available to enforce payments, less than 40% of single parents in the UK receive any maintenance from their child's other parent and those who received maintenance in 2012, whether through the CSA or by private arrangement, received an average weekly amount of only around £45 per family (not per child). Of single parents receiving child maintenance exclusively through the CSA, 40% received less than £10 per week, 38% received between £10 and £50 per week and 22% received more than £50 per week.

When resident parents receive less maintenance than they should, it is not always because their ex-partners refuse to pay what they owe or because agencies fail to take action to ensure payment. Sometimes it is because the agency's original calculations of what should be paid were incorrect. There are many unfortunate fathers who, having made regular payments of exactly what they were told they owed, suddenly hear that the level of payment was inadequate from the beginning and they now face accumulated arrears. To avoid this it is probably wise to check the claim made on you for child maintenance using one of several do-it-yourself calculators available on the internet. If the claim seems low, don't gratefully assume that it is correct: query it with the agency or your solicitor.

Some parents are surprised to discover that child maintenance and access are not legally connected. Fathers often feel that paying maintenance gives them the right to see the children, when in fact the children have a right to see their fathers whether they pay maintenance or not. Likewise many mothers whose exes do not pay the maintenance that is due from them are taken aback when they find that they cannot use non-payment as a reason to deny or limit fathers' access, or use the threat of denying access to force them to pay. The vital point for both parents to remember is that children are the subjects rather than the objects of both maintenance money and access visits. The money is not paid by the father to the mother for *her* benefit but for the child's. And access visits are not a father's privilege which he must earn or can lose, but a child's right.

4.5 Legal issues

In order to embark on divorcing, or dissolving a civil partnership, you have to apply to the Family Court and show that you have arranged where (and with whom) the children will live, how much access to them the non-resident parent will have and who will pay for their maintenance.

Working these things out between you will save a great deal of stress, time and, above all, money. Financial assistance that you were expecting – perhaps because divorced friends told you about it – will probably not be forthcoming. In the UK the government has cut legal aid for much of family law as part of spending reductions, and divorce will not be eligible for legal aid unless it is being sought because of child abuse or domestic violence.

Changes to legal aid in the UK

Until April 2013, people who were eligible for legal aid (see below) could receive its assistance to cover all aspects of family law, including divorce, disputes between unmarried partners and the dissolution of civil partnerships, financial disputes, property disputes and disputes over arrangements for children.

Now, following the Legal Aid, Sentencing and Punishment of Offenders Act (LASPO) of 2012, legal aid is no longer available for private family law problems unless there is public interest in the case, usually because there is evidence of domestic abuse or the risk of it, or there are child protection issues.

If you are eligible for legal aid you will receive it only in matters of:

- public family law regarding child protection (i.e. care proceedings)
- private family law where there is evidence of child abuse
- child abduction or the threat of it
- representation of children in private family cases
- forced marriage protection orders
- legal advice in support of mediation
- domestic violence injunction cases.

Changes to eligibility & to the scope of legal aid

Qualifications for legal aid have changed.

Previously, receipt of a passporting benefit – income support, income-related support and employment allowance, income-based jobseekers allowance, guarantee credit part of pension credit, universal credit – automatically rendered the individual eligible. Now an assessment of capital is also made and the size of the recipient's contributions has been increased.

Seeking mediation

If you are both willing to try to come to an agreement but
find it impossible to make plans together that will really stick,
mediation may help. Mediation is not legal advice (although a
court may instruct you to seek it), and it is not counselling; it is
designed to help people sort out their differences for themselves
and reach genuine agreement. Mediation will not focus on
resolving emotional issues or relationship breakdown but on
practical matters. The mediator, who will neither take sides
nor tell you what to do, meets with the two of you, usually for
several weekly sessions, and encourages you to set out your
disagreements openly and honestly and resolve them yourselves.
Mediation seldom works unless both of you genuinely want
to reach agreement; but provided you do want to, it is often
effective even if your views were poles apart at the beginning.
Mediation is not free but it is usually considerably less expensive
than taking legal advice. Make sure you ask about costs before
you begin.

Negotiating through a solicitor

If an impartial mediator cannot help you to reach joint decisions,
especially if you feel that you are being bullied or threatened
towards an 'agreement' you don't want to accept, you may
need a solicitor to help you negotiate, and if one of you has a
solicitor the other parent will need to have his own. Choose
carefully though. Some people report that the involvement of
legal professionals and the courts contributed more to chaos
than to calm in children's lives. Certainly the adversarial system
legal professionals represent and work within can make for an
atmosphere of unrelenting hostility, even aggression, between
separating parents, so that even if you are trying to co-operate
for the children's good their involvement makes that more
difficult. Around the family courts and associated offices it
sometimes seems that there is more discussion of what is 'fair'
to women and what is 'fair' to men than there is about what
will be best for individual children. When it comes to children's
living arrangements and contact with the non-resident parent,
you may be the only ones paying attention to what will work
for younger children or being prepared to listen to what older
children want.

In order to reduce the adversarial atmosphere that tends to
surround these negotiations, a growing minority of solicitors is
practising what is referred to as 'collaborative law' in which you
and your ex-partner meet and discuss your differences face-
to-face, as you might do in mediation, but with the important

difference that each of you has your own solicitor present at each meeting. Unlike a mediator each solicitor will provide his or her client with support and advice, but unlike traditional practice in which solicitors work against each other, they will work together in the interests of helping the two of you reach mutual agreements.

When you have found a solicitor you find sympathetic, make sure you understand the likely costs before you ask him or her to act on your behalf. Some solicitors (including some practising collaborative law) offer 'fixed fee family law services' in which the costs of each stage of your case are laid down in advance. This makes it much easier to budget. Without such an arrangement, costs that accumulate outside visits – for phone calls, for example, or for photocopying and posting documents to your ex's solicitor – can be unexpected and surprisingly high. Unlike a mediator, a solicitor who is not practising collaborative law will be on the side of the person who employs him or her (which is why each of you may want to employ your own). It is the individual who sought the consultation and will pay the bill whose rights and options will be addressed. When you have decided which of these options you want to pursue, your solicitor will negotiate on your behalf with your ex's solicitor, probably by making phone calls and exchanging letters.

Whether you and your partner iron out your disagreements between yourselves or with the help of a mediator or a solicitor, your agreement will only be legally binding once you have obtained a 'consent order'. Drafted by a solicitor and signed in draft by both of you, a 'consent order' is a legally binding document that confirms your detailed agreement concerning financial affairs, property and child maintenance. Do make sure that your consent order is ratified by the court. There have been cases in which agreements were left in draft, leaving them open to being re-addressed by one of the parties who, sometimes years later, saw a possibility of improving his or her settlement.

If negotiation fails

If you and your ex cannot agree on arrangements for your children even after a mediator, or solicitors working collaboratively, have tried to help you, you may have to apply to the court to decide between you on the outstanding matters.

You should be aware that this is a last resort and in no way an easy option. Without access to legal aid you may find it impossible to afford legal representation and may have to represent yourself.

Furthermore, in the UK, a bill passed in April 2014 introduces a new family court. This bill has reformed legislation and reduced court involvement in a wide range of issues relating to families and young people, which may complicate your access to and use of the court.

Among its key points:

- It makes extra provision to encourage mediation in family disputes, and sets out the circumstances under which anyone who is trying to start court proceedings in a family law matter may be instructed to attend a mediation information and assessment meeting before the application can even be considered.
- The bill sets out a clear statement of courts' presumption that when parents separate it is in any child's best interests to have both parents involved in his or her life unless the contrary is shown. This is intended to reduce the possibility of one parent using court proceedings to punish or exclude the other.
- That presumption does not hold if there are issues around child protection or domestic violence. However, no case showing that involvement with both parents is *not* in the child's interests can be made on the basis of fears or suspicions. A parent who wishes to bring such a case to court – with or without any legal aid for which, under these exceptional circumstances, they might be eligible – will have to supply evidence that she or he is a victim of domestic violence or that child abuse has taken place, and that she or he is divorcing or separating from an abusive partner.

Asking the court to decide

Family courts deal with parental disputes over the upbringing of children, local authority intervention to protect children, decrees relating to divorce, financial support for children after divorce or relationship breakdown, and some aspects of domestic violence and adoption.

You can apply for a single court order, or a number of them, depending on which issues remain outstanding between the two of you. The court will make a particular order if, and only if, it considers that the results of the order would be better for the child than the status quo, and this is usually the case. Bear in mind, though, that the order you get may not be the order you hoped for. Once you have applied to the court in this way it will do what it considers best for the child.

A child's mother, father or anyone with parental responsibility can apply for a court order. Other people, such as grandparents, can also apply for these court orders if they first get permission from the court.

Making an application to the court

Whoever is making the application to the court must complete a form stating the reason for the application. The court will set a date for the application to be heard and may ask CAFCASS (Children and Family Court Advisory and Support Service – the independent organisation which looks after the interests of children in family proceedings) for its input. If CAFCASS is involved it should send you information about its role and the court process. CAFCASS will try to speak to you and the other parent before the court hearing to find out more about the situation, and may also contact your local council and other services such as the police to see if they hold any information that might show safety or welfare concerns about your children. CAFCASS will write to the court before the first hearing telling them about the work they have done and advising the court on what it considers to be in the children's best interests.

The first hearing

Usually, parents, any legal advisers, an officer from CAFCASS (in Wales CAFCASS officers are called family court advisers) and a district judge will attend the first hearing. Any particular problems will be discussed and the judge will try to reach a quick agreement. If an agreement is reached at the first hearing, the court can decide whether or not to make an order immediately, confirming arrangements.

After the first hearing

If an agreement has not been reached at the first hearing, the court may require you and the non-resident parent to attend a meeting about mediation, or a separated parents information programme.

The court may decide to arrange another hearing for a later date, allowing time for more evidence to be gathered and a report prepared. The court may ask for an assessment of the family dynamics and the children's relationships with each parent by an Expert Witness, or it may ask for more evidence and a report from CAFCASS who as part of their report will talk to your children, if they are considered old enough, about their wishes and feelings.

The children and families bill has just become law and changes to part 2 – Family Justice – are not yet fully implemented. Issues addressed by such orders are unlikely to change but the orders that are most commonly applied for will be called "child arrangement orders" so as to focus attention on children's needs rather than parents' rights. This grouping will include orders currently called:

- **a residence order**, which sets out where and with whom a child should live;
- **a contact order**, which lays down the amount of contact the non-resident parent should have with the child, how contact should be made and, if necessary, where this contact should take place. If a court, social worker or solicitor decides that the non-resident parent might harm either the child or the resident parent during ordinary contact, or might seek to kidnap the child, an order may be made for the non-resident parent to meet with the child only in the neutral environment of a contact centre.

As well as parents or guardians, partners in a marriage or civil partnership that constituted the child's family (such as step-parents) or anyone the child has been living with for at least three of the last five years can apply to the court for contact. With the permission of the court, grandparents, other relatives and the child themselves can also apply.

- **A specific issue order**, which is used when there is disagreement about particular aspects of children's upbringing, such as what school they go to or whether they should have a religious education.
- **A prohibited steps order (PSO)**, which is used to prevent the non-resident parent from making decisions about the child's upbringing which they would otherwise be entitled to make as part of normal parental responsibility. For example, a non-resident father may be prohibited from taking a child on holiday or abroad, or taking him to spend time with another adult who is considered unsuitable.

The existence of such an order also means that the resident parent can go ahead and make important and urgent decisions on the child's behalf – such as those concerning medical treatment – without first seeking the agreement of the other parent.

Enforcing court orders

If you disagree with the terms of a court order you may be able to appeal against it. Appealing is difficult and complicated and you will need legal advice which will be expensive. However, appealing against an order is definitely preferable to breaching it.

Contact centres

Contact centres are designed to provide a child-friendly environment that is not in either parent's home. Contact centres are often held in places such as local community centres or church halls. A typical centre will be open twice each week and staffed by volunteers. Many will charge a fee for their services.

When parents attend contact centres it is usually because a court has decided that direct and unsupervised contact might carry a risk of harm, either to the child or to the parent with care. Social workers, solicitors and CAFCASS officers can also make referrals independently. In some circumstances, parents can themselves arrange to use a contact centre, perhaps as a safe and neutral place where they can hand the children over for contact visits without themselves having to meet. However, there is a shortage of contact centres in many areas so there are often limits on who can use them and how often.

Visits that take place in a contact centre are called 'supervised contact' and there are some contact centres that specialise in providing professional, or at least skilled, supervision. What is usually provided, though, is more accurately described as 'supported contact', which means that there will be volunteers around who will generally oversee all visits taking place, making sure children are safe and adults behave appropriately, but nobody supervising individual contact arrangements. Speak to staff beforehand to find out what type of service is offered and what it will be like.

More information available from Gingerbread:
www.gingerbread.org.uk

Part II

Separating Better – Or Worse

5 Keeping parenting & partnership apart

There are almost as many ways of coping or failing to cope with parental separation and divorce as there are parents separating, and no book can sensibly suggest which will feel best, or least horrible, to you. However, it does seem that from the point of view of children – children in general, not specifically yours – there are better and worse ways of handling it, emotionally and practically. All the positive ways go together and so do all the negative ways. If (almost) everything you say and do for your children, and the arrangements you make for them, now and months or years ahead, fit with the 'better' group, you're making good choices. If a lot of it fits under 'worse', you're not.

The very best way to manage the break-up of a family with minimal long-term harm to children is to set yourselves to support the relationships each of you has with each of your children, and protect them from the failure of the relationship between the two of you. That's not an easy thing to do, and if you are a mother (or father) reading this when you are almost overwhelmed with hurt and fury at the children's father (or mother), it may seem downright impossible. Some people do manage it, though, and it is the most important effort you can make for your children right now because it will affect every aspect of their lives both during and after your separation and divorce.

Whatever you are feeling about your soon-to-be ex as a husband or partner it is, and should be, irrelevant to what your children feel about him as their father. He's never going to be 'ex' to them (the two of you may be getting divorced but he's not divorcing the children). And even if you think he is a bit rubbish as a dad, your children don't. To them he's just daddy. He's the only father they know and, bitter though it may be for you to acknowledge it right now, they love him as they love you. Each child has two beloved parents. You're going to be a lone parent but that need not, and should not, mean that your children are going to be motherless or fatherless.

Feeling motherless or fatherless is – literally – terrible for a child of any age (see Chapter 1), but watching a parent struggling with the sadness, anger and depression of separation is also miserable

for him or her. Many people believe that children don't notice or
care what is happening to adults, that they are only concerned
with their own feelings and aren't even aware of anyone else's.
That is a misapprehension and an important one. When children
behave in ways that seem thoughtless, it is often because of
their immaturity. Young children don't go on playing noisy games
when you've told them you have a headache because they
don't care about you, but because they haven't yet developed
the empathy which lets them put themselves in your shoes and
realise that lots of noise will make your headache worse. With
any luck they don't even really know what 'headache' means.
As children get older their seemingly endless demands for
your attention, even when you are on the phone or watching
something on TV, are not because they are spoiled and care only
about themselves, but because you are so much the centre of
their lives that they find it hard to believe that they are not the
entire centre of yours.

Children of all ages are extremely sensitive to parents' moods
and feelings. The cues a baby uses are not the same as an
older child's, of course, and the understanding a four-year-old
brings to what is going on is not the same as an adolescent's,
but whatever their age your child will sense when either
or both of you are unhappy and distracted, or irritated and
enraged with each other, and will worry about you both. Just
as bereaved children mourn differently from adults and are
sometimes thought to be heartless, children show this kind
of worry in different ways from adults. Your son is as likely to
bring you an extra-large beetle to stroke as to stroke your arm.
But, however childish concern is expressed, it's important to
recognise it so that you do what you can to reassure children
that you are basically OK. You won't be able to conceal your
feelings altogether. And you can't reassure children by trying to
pretend that everything about the family is fine when it is not;
nothing will confuse them more than having you tell them one
thing when they clearly sense another. So while trying to keep
household routines ordinary, and taking the trouble not to say
nasty disparaging things about each other in a child's hearing
(on the phone or to a friend as well as face-to-face) will be a good
start, it isn't enough.

To make the best of what is inevitably a bad situation for the
child, each of you needs to make a clear separation in your mind
and in your behaviour between the adult-to-adult and the
adult-to-child relationships in the family. Managing to keep
partner and parent relationships separate means that when you
are with a child you won't display the negative feelings that
belong to your relationship as woman-to-man because they

don't belong to her relationship as child-to-father. If (and when) you can manage that, your child will know that the unhappiness she sees and senses is only adult business; the parenting business that is central to her life is still intact.

The brief quote to the right makes it tragically clear that this father has *not* managed to separate his relationship with his wife from his child's relationship with her. At that point in the family upheaval he felt that he and his little daughter had been equally 'left' and that the loss of love for himself that led to the separation included the child. 'She can't love her the way I do' is not a good starting point for mutual parenting. In contrast, the following quote is.

Father of girl aged 4

" Yes, I know she loves her too. And Izzie loves her mum come to that. But she can't love her the way I do or she wouldn't have walked out would she? They say it's really rare for mothers to scarper and if one parent walks out it's usually the dad, but I'd never, never have done that. Never. "

Even those few words suggest a fundamental difference between the relationships of the two couples. The father who is quoted first feels that he and his little daughter are both victims in the separation: both were 'left'. The mother who is quoted second, on the other hand, sees the marital break-up as separate business and being left in the home as the next step both parents thought best for the child.

Keeping parenting apart from partnership is somewhat easier when you realise that whatever their ages, children don't want to share or even hear about parents' man-to-woman relationships. They may love to hear stories about how you met, or the drive to hospital the night they were born, but they will resist and resent being made to recognise and think about your emotional, and especially your sexual, life with each other. That relationship is adult business, not children's. The feelings that go with a breaking marriage are not something they are ready for themselves and hearing too much about it can splash embarrassment around the parental relationships also. Using a child as a confidante is at best inappropriate, at worst sometimes close to abusive:

Girl aged 12

" When we were at his house dad did talk – would talk – about him and mum and how much he missed her and how she'd betrayed him. It didn't make me sorry for him, it made me embarrassed, especially when it looked as if he was going to cry. One time he'd been drinking whisky and he got all emotional and started talking about getting lonely for her in bed. Yuck. That put me off both of them. "

The disintegration of your marriage or committed partnership will certainly be bad for your children whatever you do, but if you want to protect them from the very worst of it, you'll both do all you can to keep your hurt, sense of betrayal, loneliness and fury private from them, and keep the arguments and fights that belong to your adult and sexual relationship, not to their child-to-parent relationships, as quiet as you can.

Almost as difficult and even more important, you'll struggle to prevent what you feel about the person who broke up the partnership from changing what you've always felt about him or her as a parent. If the man who has left you, was an OK dad before your adult relationship blew up, he still will be if circumstances (and you) allow him. If he's always been an active parent, loving and hands on, you need to go on believing in his absolute reliability as a father, respecting his input into every aspect of the child's upbringing and enjoying their pleasure in each other. It isn't easy, but it is possible, especially if both of you feel at least some degree of joint responsibility for the separation and if there isn't a third party closely involved. It's difficult enough to be positive about your child spending the weekend with the other parent, much more difficult if there's a substitute-you there too (see Chapter 3.4).

When separating parents do manage to salvage intact not only their own but each other's parenting, they sometimes find that part of the lonely space left by the broken partnership has been filled with mutual parenting. That's the best possible gift they can make to their children.

Mother of two boys aged 4 and 8

His second affair threw up a lot or crap between us but even before it had settled I realised that he was still the only person in the world I could trust with the boys, the only person who'd drop everything for them in any kind of emergency and handle it, whatever it was, just the way I'd want. I had other people supporting me as a lone mum, but I'd think about dying, and what would happen to Luke and Larry if I did, and the thought of them going to live with their grandmother or one of their aunts gave me the absolute shudders. Their father is the only other person they 100% love and who would bring them up the way we'd planned. So I didn't want him for me – let's face it, didn't want him in my bed any more – but I did want him for our children and that's dictated all our arrangements ever since.

Father of girl aged 2 during the divorce, and now aged 5

If Diane had been older maybe we'd have tried separate flats close by so she could pop in and out. But with her so little we weren't going to divide her up, so we divided ourselves up: split the house. We have half each, she has it all. Lots of people, like neighbours who aren't real friends, don't even know we're divorced. Diane knows of course but it really doesn't bother her. Why should it? There's always a parent at home and there're always supper in one of two kitchens and her own precious bed waiting in her room.

5.1 Mutual parenting

Mutual parenting is not at all the same as shared or equal parenting. Those terms usually refer to arrangements in which a child's time (and therefore care) is shared between mother and father and is dealt with in Chapter 7.

Mutual parenting means that whatever else is or is not going on in your relationships with each other – today, this month or next year – you are jointly committed to putting your children's wellbeing and happiness first and to protecting them as far as you can from ill-effects following your separation. The most important word in that sentence is 'jointly'. Many separating mothers say that they put their children first, and many fathers say that they do too, but not many of them credit each other with doing so or manage to do it together.

The most difficult aspect of making your children's wellbeing a mutual priority is that it involves you in being together, or at least in frequent communication, when you'd probably prefer to have nothing whatsoever to do with each other. What is more, if you are very bitter towards your ex you may find that although you are sure of your own commitment and good intentions towards the children, you struggle to believe in those of a person you are currently finding it impossible to tolerate or trust, let alone like. It is a worthwhile struggle, though, because conflict between the parents is known to be the very worst aspect of many children's experience of family breakdown: they suffer more from your enmity than from the actual separation.

Even leaving aside the stress of having to be in touch with an ex-partner, putting children first doesn't come easily to all separating parents – or to all parents in intact families, come to that. Seeing divorce as the way out of a marriage that's become miserable, some feel that they are entitled to make seeking their own happiness their priority.

Everyone is entitled to look for their own happiness, provided that happiness does not come at a disproportionately high cost to someone else. So while of course parents are entitled to seek their own happiness with or without new partners (greater happiness for at least one person is the point of separating, after all), they are surely not entitled to allow their separation and seeking to cost their children one iota more misery than it need to. Parents (and indeed all adults) need to put children ahead of themselves, not only because it's nicer for children to be happy but also because children's happiness and wellbeing affects the kind of people they will grow up to be and therefore the kind of society they will make when it's time for them to take over.

Mother of girl aged 2

" *It goes without saying that she matters and of course I'll see she's OK, but I don't see that she has to come first. This divorce is for me, to free me to be with someone I really love.* "

A pledge for children

> *We must put children first because we are all children first. The children we were, the children we have now and the children they may have in the future are not our possessions or burdens: they are all of us. Children's wellbeing is the key to a society that is good for everyone so ensuring it is everybody's responsibility and in everybody's interests.*

Mindful Policy Group: www.mindful policy group.com

As well as each making your responsibilities as parents your priority, you need to agree what those responsibilities are. They don't have to be the same for each of you. Many fathers and mothers have played very different roles in their children's lives during the marriage and if that's how married parenting worked, divorced but mutual parenting may work similarly – or very differently. Being equally responsible as parents doesn't have to mean equality in practical arrangements for sharing the children's time and care, either; that's a different issue (see Chapter 7). One way or another, though, those joint responsibilities will have to include making it possible – and enjoyable – for children to be closely in touch with each parent and, unless there is a devastatingly good reason against it, to spend time with the non-resident parent. Missing out on having a close relationship with each of you is exactly the kind of separation damage you are trying to protect them from.

If you are having trouble deciding whether you can manage mutual parenting, whether, for the children's sakes, you can each stand to be in co-operative touch rather than walking away from each other as well as from the marriage, don't rush. Give yourselves time to get over the shock of separation and then ask yourselves whether each of you would do as much to help the other with your joint children as you would do to help your sister or your best friend with hers.

- Would you phone him/expect him to phone you in the middle of the night if there was an emergency, such as one child needing to be taken to hospital and there being no one to care for the others?
- Would you discuss with him/expect him to discuss with you any worrying child behaviour, such as a three-year-old going back to nappies or a nine-year-old crying easily and often?
- Would you do your best/expect him to do his best to make the transfer from one parent to the other at the beginning and end of visits easy for the children?

Mother of three girls all under 5

> *Yes, I do think separating is right for us but I also think that we are only entitled to do it if we can protect the kids from the fallout. In fact (does this sound horribly pi?) I think we've sort of got to earn the end of our marriage by making sure of their parenting.*

- Would you cover for him/expect him to cover for you if one
  of you had forgotten a child's sports day or school play
  and didn't turn up ('mummy had to work late' rather than
  'mummy forgot')?
- Would you pay attention to each other's views on important
  educational decisions such as keeping a child in preschool
  for an extra year, choosing a school, finding the money for a
  school trip or taking up a musical instrument?
- Would you pay attention to each other's views on managing
  children's behaviour (such as how best to handle tantrums
  or how much fuss to make about table manners), and try to
  agree on routines (such as bedtimes) and limits (such as not
  cycling without a helmet) so that the children met similar
  expectations and boundaries with each parent?

If the answer to all or most of those is 'yes' (or 'of course', 'no
question' or 'what do you *think?*') then you do have the
foundations for mutual parenting.

A parent doesn't have to have been hands-on with the children
to make parenting responsibilities a priority, although he may
become more hands-on when he suddenly finds himself in
full charge, and his relationships with the children will change
anyway as they get older. But while mutual parenting within an
intact family can work on the basis of different gender roles –
accepted by both parents and by the children – mutual parenting
after a separation does require at least enough blurring of those
roles that each parent can operate independently of the other.
Above all it is difficult to make separated parenting mutual
unless interest in the children is mutual. Giving equal headspace
to the children is more important than being equally hands-on.
A man whose fathering has been conventional/old-fashioned
may have had very little practise at changing nappies, but as
long as he realises that it matters to the toddler how nappies
are changed, he can soon learn. The issue, as the points above
suggest, is child-centredness.

The mother quoted here found
it difficult to imagine her
children's father becoming
child-centred and it's easy to
see why. But although they
started from different points of
view and with very different
attitudes, these two *almost*
managed successful mutual
parenting.

Mother of two girls aged 5 and 7, and a boy aged 9

" Mark is a man's man. He likes women as playmates
and kids for status. I've never known him put the
children ahead of his own wishes, in fact finding time to
spend with them among his work and the tennis club
was rare, and he always wanted me to make babysitting
arrangements so we could have adults-only holidays
or evenings out. He really doesn't like family treats or
celebrations. In fact I don't think he's really a family
man, so how can I take him seriously when he says all
the divorce business must put the kids first? "

The father, Mark, responded by saying that he felt that his main responsibility as a parent was to make generous and secure financial arrangements after the divorce. He planned to play a part in the children's lives by sharing decisions about their education and activities. He also assumed that once his ex was a lone parent it would be his responsibility to provide emergency back-up, although he reserved the right to do that 'by throwing my money at it rather than my time'. Although he had never seen much of the children he did realise that he was no longer even glimpsing them at the breakfast table and he was looking for other ways of seeing them regularly within his own lifestyle. His most successful initiative was taking them for lessons at the tennis club each weekend, which they much enjoyed.

However, after more than a year it gradually became clear that mutual parenting wasn't working for Mark and his ex, and the aspect which ended up being out of reach was the part that makes it work best: mother and father feeling genuinely supportive of each other in relation to the children and even retaining some respect for each other as parents. The children's mother had never respected Mark as a father and he had little respect for the role of mother. After two or three years they had to settle for the next best thing, which is polite parenting.

5.2 Polite parenting

Some couples who understand the importance to children of their parents staying in close touch nevertheless find it impossible to achieve – or even imagine – the two-way support that is the essence of mutual parenting. Fortunately, being unable wholeheartedly to support each other doesn't mean you have to be enemies. There are lesser degrees of contact and communication that demand much less friendship but still protect the children from the worst fall-out from the parental separation-bomb.

Starting polite parenting usually depends on making relatively formal arrangements, not only about dividing up money and property and about which parent the child will live with after separation, but also about when and where and how the other parent will spend time with him. Since before a court will grant you a divorce or dissolve a civil partnership you have to show that you have made these arrangements you have to discuss them (see Chapter 4). And if you are both trying to be polite you may be able to work them out between you. Often, though, parents who are struggling with civility enlist the help of solicitors to make sure that these agreements leave nothing to chance (or to unwelcome discussion).

Rigid plans backed by written documents can only be the bare bones of life after separation, though. Some couples draw up amazingly detailed documents, including lists of rules to which each signs agreement, templates for telephone calls between them and 'visit logs' which each parent must fill in each time the child is transferred to the care of the other. But while drawing up documents such as these may make it easier for parents who can hardly bring themselves to speak to each other to talk about their children, actually using them is likely to provide one parent with a weapon to use against the other ('It says you're to bring her back by six thirty, not six forty-seven') and the hope must be that they won't be needed for long. Once you have been physically apart for a few months, during which time neither of you has broken the agreements nor done anything to offend, the flexibility you need and the communication it takes can usually creep in. It's not unheard of for a polite parenting set-up eventually to become something close to mutual.

Sometimes, though, parents have issues with each other that make even polite parenting impossible. Perhaps, for example, a father is determined to have easy access to a small child and 'fair shares of her time', despite the fact that while the marriage lasted his fathering was of the 'bedtime story when he got home early enough' kind.

If a father has never before taken sole responsibility for his child – meals and play, bath times, bedtimes and bad dreams, squabbles and safety measures – it is understandable if the mother finds it impossible to agree to any overnight visits until he has got to know the child. If he is determined not to 'settle for anything less', even for a few months, any attempts at co-operation may fail.

Some fathers and mothers have always had different views on aspects of their children's upbringing. While they lived together one parent balanced the other and their differences didn't seem insurmountable, but once they are apart neither parent can feel fully supportive and trusting of the other:

Father of girl aged 3

> *Come on Maria, you've always played up what hard work it is looking after Melanie, but how hard can it be?*

Father of two boys aged 3 and 4, and one girl aged 8

> *There are things to do with the kids that we just don't agree on. Like she's really against ordinary medicine and into all that alternative stuff. We've often argued about it and a few times I've actually taken one of them to the GP against her wishes 'cause I thought he needed antibiotics. What will happen when I'm not around?*

Mother of girl aged 4

> *He's a good father but he's nobody's darling daddy. Bit uptight. Bit cold. Very religious. He never interfered with the way I carried on with her but she'll not get much fun or much loving if I'm not there.*

Being polite is even more difficult for a parent who feels that the other is (or might be) a negative influence in a child's life. For example, if one parent has always found it difficult to meet or even tolerate a child's special needs, the other parent may not even want to contemplate situations where parent and child are alone together.

Mother of boy aged 6

> *When Charles was a baby his father could cope. But changing nappies on 'a big boy' and helping him feed himself with a spoon is beyond him. He says it turns him up and I've always done it. If the two of them were alone together I don't think he'd leave Charles dirty or hungry, but I do think he'd make it obvious he was disgusted and I wouldn't trust him not to try and force Charles to do things that are beyond him.*

These are not the kinds of issue that both parents are likely to reach agreement on without help, but that doesn't mean they have to cause a fight. If a basic plan is arrived at, with help, perhaps, from a mediator or a solicitor, such that the children will live with the father in the first example, the mother in the other two, and in each instance have daytime (rather than overnight) contact at weekends with the other parent, there is no reason why arrangements between the parents for putting the plan into action should not remain polite. If even that kind of agreement seems out of reach because both parents want to be the 'parent with care' or at least to have the child stay with them over weekends or holidays, or one parent wants to leave the country, taking the children with them, it is still worth attending a mediation information and assessment meeting to see if you can work things out between you without going to court.

It is when you cannot work things out even with the help of a mediator, or when the situation is more difficult still because it involves domestic violence or abuse, seen by or perhaps suffered by the child, that legal advice and court orders will be necessary (see Chapter 4.5).

6 Trying to get children to take sides

6.1 What 'alienation' means & why it matters

The very worst thing you can do to your children during the horrible months around your separation is to try to put them off the other parent. You'll hear this called 'alienation' by solicitors or social workers and in court. Now that we know how important it is for children to be as closely involved as possible with both parents, alienation is recognised as dreadfully damaging. In some parts of the world, including the United States, it is actually against the law for one parent to set out to spoil a child's relationship with, or feelings about, the other.

When a parent sets out to alienate a child from the other parent, he or she is usually enmeshed in angry estrangement between spouses that is not being kept apart from the relationships between parents and children. Deliberate alienation uses children as weapons in an adult battle, making them even more its victims. From children's point of view this is the most damaging, the worst way their mothers and fathers can react to separation and it leads to the very opposite of the best: to 'broken parenting' instead of to 'mutual' or even 'polite parenting'.

6.2 Alienation by circumstance or by default

Avoiding 'broken parenting' is at least as difficult as achieving 'mutual parenting', and for the same reasons: adults' feelings about each other messing up their feelings for their children.

If you're a mother or father whose partner has left the family home, it's all too easy to put your child off him or her even without meaning to. You are upset, miserable, furious – whatever your exact emotions they are probably pretty strong – and however hard you try to conceal your feelings your child will sense them. Because you are there and the child is upset because his father or mother is not, he may well take your side, turning against your soon-to-be ex. That scenario is especially likely if, far from being part of a long process of marriage breakdown with one parent's eventual departure mutually anticipated if not exactly agreed, the separation was a shock to you and you still hope, or at least wish, that the marriage may be glued together again. Children almost invariably want that too, so that puts the two of you on the same side (and in the same house) with the other parent on the other side and somewhere else.

Boy aged 6, when asked 'What made you so angry with your dad?', answered:

> *Mum kept crying. She cried a lot. I hated her crying. And dad wasn't ever there to huggle her better. And when I said to her 'let's go and get him' she said 'he just doesn't want to be here any more' and I'm here so that meant he didn't want to be with me either.*

If the break-up was over an affair, your child will soon gather that and may not easily forgive what he or she will probably see as a straightforward theft of one parent from the other. Children who need to blame someone find it far easier to blame an individual who isn't either parent but a cuckoo in the family nest. If the relationship that tips your marriage into separation should prove long-lasting, establishing a good relationship between the parent's new lover and the children may be bedevilled by their continued resentment. Meantime, the parent who has been left alone will almost always attract more of a child's (and everyone else's) sympathy so unless you really work to prevent it (see Chapter 5) the whole situation will push the children and their other parent apart.

It is miserably easy for a baby or toddler to become alienated from a parent who isn't there – let's say it's her father who has left because the statistics say that's more likely than her mother – just *because* he isn't there. Unless the two of you make a point of father and child seeing each other regularly and often from the very beginning of the separation, their relationship will loosen and eventually lapse. If one of you actually wants that to happen – perhaps because the father wants to leave the whole family behind him and make a 'new life' or because you want to punish him, or perhaps because neither of you wants anything whatsoever to do with the other – all you have to do is keep them mostly apart for several months. A shockingly large number of confused angry women do just that, perhaps not realising that their beloved child who has done nothing wrong suffers at least as much as her dad.

If a baby, under a year old, doesn't spend any time with her father for weeks or months, the attachment between them that should have been building up towards a peak in the second year doesn't grow. She will not 'forget' him. Whatever relationship she had with her father while he lived in the same home played a part in the way her brain and nervous system developed in her first months (see Chapter 2.1) so he is forever part of who she is. But the area of her brain that stores memories is not yet developed enough for her consciously to remember him for long. If he is out of sight for months he will also be out of conscious mind. She will not be aware of missing him because the space in her life that he used to occupy will close up.

It's different if a child is two or three years old when the break-up happens. If he has made a close bond with the father during his short life before the separation, he will be very aware of father's departure and absence and at the beginning will probably badly miss specific things they used to do together. But over a few months he will get used to his father not being there and adapt to the new lifestyle. If a reconciliation brought daddy home he would probably still be delighted, but suddenly being expected to leave mum and home and go out with him (perhaps because the father has gained legal access) is a different matter. Daddy doesn't mean anything clear-cut to him. In fact, he may not really understand who this man is. He may be shy and reluctant. A toddler's very natural hanging back – probably with both arms firmly around his mother's thigh – is a potent weapon in an undeclared alienation war. His father, who was looking forward to excited greetings and hugs from his child, will feel devastatingly sad and rejected, especially if he has been fighting hard for the right to spend time with him. His mother will probably feel vindicated, or at least excused for her part in keeping them apart. Clearly the child does not want to be with the father, and surely he should not be forced? By the time that question gets back to conciliation or court another few weeks, even months, will have passed and that child, now three years old, has little remaining conscious memory of this man.

Yet another year or two on, at four or five, that shyness with a scarcely-known visiting father and reluctance to go with him may take on a desperate intensity, with the child tearful and panicky when the father comes to pick her up. The extreme reaction is usually not to being with the father but to being taken away from the mother. Look at it from the child's point of view: daddy left, so how can she be sure that if she takes her eyes off mummy she won't leave too (see Chapter 8)?

A scene like that is agony for everybody. For the child, who is submerged in the worst kind of fear there is for a child that age: fear of losing her mother. For the mother, who hates to see her so upset (and hates the father for making her that way) and of course for father who is being made to feel like an insensitive brute for wanting to spend time with the daughter he loves. Probably nobody meant father and child to become alienated, but they have.

If a child's relationship with his or her father is protected and facilitated from the beginning, even though the two of them don't live in the same house any more (see Chapter 5), painful separation scenes like this can usually be avoided. But not always. Separation anxiety is ordinary in one- to three-year-olds and by no means unusual for another two or three years, especially when family stresses make children feel insecure (see Chapter 8). But if it is not unusual for 'contact arrangements' to blow up, it is vital not to abandon contact altogether. For babies, toddlers and preschool children there is one particular solution that's guaranteed from a child's point of view, though it can be tough on parents: let her father come to the child's home to spend time with her and, if necessary, have mum hanging around in the background so she feels safe.

Understandable though the feelings of the mother quoted here may be, they belong to the mother's relationship as woman-to-man, not to Mary's relationship with her father. Some agreed grown-up ground rules might help in situations like these. For example, you might agree that child and father stay downstairs or in the bit of the home where she normally plays; that he uses the downstairs bathroom and doesn't go upstairs; and that he only gets cups of tea if you offer.

If you really cannot bring yourself to let your ex spend time in the home even though you can see that it's the best way for your small child to spend happy time with him, a compromise may work. If there is a grandparent, aunt or friend the child feels close to, and whose house she often visits, meeting her father there may enable her to enjoy being with him. Meeting at her grandmother's house worked for Mary, and when grandmother went away on holiday Mary and her father were made welcome by Lucy's mum.

'Enjoy' is the key point, of course. If going out with dad floods a child with anxiety and she is more or less forced to go, she will get minimal pleasure from this visit and, remembering her own anxious feelings, may dread the next. On the other hand, the more she enjoys whatever time she spends with her father and looks forward to seeing him again, the more self-sustaining their relationship will be.

Grandmother of Mary aged 3

" *Mary's not four yet. She can't get her arms right around the pillar-box that stands outside her front gate but it's a sturdy, familiar landmark and she's going to hang on to it whatever all the grown-ups say about daddy taking her for a treat. I think she knows she's being conned. Treats have mummy in them. Or me. Or maybe Lucy's mum (she's good at treats).* "

Mary's mother

" *I couldn't have him in the house, playing with Mary as if he was still family; seeing my things; drinking my tea as if he lived there…* "

Using your child as a go-between

If you are not seeing your ex but your child is, it's very convenient to use your child as a messenger and very tempting to extract information from her. Don't. Even if you and your ex are on 'polite' terms, the messages you send are entirely practical and the questions you ask are completely casual (*How was daddy today? Was he cheerful?*), being used as a go-between mixes the child into the failed marital relationship when she ought to be allowed to think only about the successful parental one. If she wants to tell you what she's been doing, that's great (*How was your day?*), but don't ask her about her father. She'll volunteer anything she wants you to know.

When you need to communicate with your ex, just do it. That was far more difficult a generation ago than it is now. Thanks to mobiles, phoning doesn't mean being in a specific place with a landline, calling at a particular time of day, or running the risk of your ex's lover or boss picking up. If you don't want to phone because you don't want to speak to him or her, you can send a text or an email. If there are things you need to show – documents or things in catalogues you're hoping the children can have for Christmas – using Skype can save you the time and emotional effort of meeting face to face, and save you money too. However you choose to do it, your children's day-to-day wellbeing depends on the two of you being willing and able to communicate and to keep your communication between the two of you.

The less friendly, or even polite, the terms you are on the worse it is for your child to play go-between, because every message risks conveying subtle criticism. The child will pick up on that and feel that he's being forced to share it.

'Tell your dad not to forget it's your concert next Saturday' sounds harmless but isn't: it clearly suggests to the child that his father is likely to forget an event that's important to him. Almost all 'reminders' also subtly convey the superiority of the parent who sends them over the recipient. *'I know when sports day or half-term is because I'm the parent in the know; he won't know unless I tell him and won't remember unless I remind him.'*

Boy aged 14

My mum really tried not to pry, not even to ask questions when I'd been out with dad. But the atmosphere kind of stank of unasked questions and it got worse as I got older. One day – it must have been about a year ago so I'd have been 13 – I'd been out with him and when I got home mum asked if I'd had a nice time and that was OK: I said yes it had been fine. But then she asked me how my dad was and I managed to say he was fine, too. But then she tried one more question (the one she'd been building up to all along, as if I didn't realise that), how did his new job seem to be going? And I just blew up and told her 'if you really want to know ask him yourself'.

Even people who are not friends can email, so the 'if you have something to say to each other, do it directly' rule still holds (but don't forget to read through your message before you press 'send'). Do remember, though, that when it comes to keeping track of nursery or school dates and events, each of you has an equal right to be kept informed by the school. If the school still communicates via those pieces of paper that end up crumpled in the bottom of your child's bag, a copy should routinely go in the post to the non-resident parent. If it isn't happening it's because nobody has told the school that the child's two parents live apart. Do it. If the school uses email, or expects parents to watch its website, make sure the office has both addresses.

6.3 Angry alienation & its use as a weapon in adult conflict

A parent who lets a child get involved in the adult war that's raging in and around the household, or even deliberately uses her as a weapon against the other parent, probably doesn't mean their child any harm. She may be one of many women who feel that unlike being a mother, being a father is an earned privilege that men can lose through bad behaviour, and who don't think about the spin-off effects on the children. Or he may be so full of fury at the woman who has betrayed him that he thinks he's actually right to protect the child from her mother.

However well-meaning such a parent's motives, and whatever the individual circumstances, deliberate alienation is wrong, and the lengths to which some alienating parents will go and the damage they cause to their children are truly shocking.

When a father has left the family home some mothers will lie and cheat to keep him and their child from speaking to or seeing each other, and to lessen the father in the child's eyes:

> To the father: *He can't come to the phone he's in the bath.*
> To the child: *No it was not your father. Do you really think he's going to bother phoning?*
> To the father: *She told me to tell you she doesn't want to speak to you.*
> To the child: *Yes it was him. Drunk as per usual. I told him he wasn't fit to speak to you.*
> To the father on doorstep: *They're not coming out with you; they've gone to their nan's.*
> To the children: *You didn't want to go with him and leave me all by myself did you?*

Examples such as these may sound trivial but cumulatively they are toxic.

Some parents, men as well as women, will share their own hateful feelings with children, encouraging them not only to see the absent one in a bad light now, but also to lose faith in the family relationships they used to take for granted:

> *She's never been any good; I never would have married her 'cept you was on the way. She's nothing of a mum. Yes, of course you thought you loved her but that's where she's clever. She turns on the charm and people believe it.*

Perhaps cruellest of all, some parents play a bid for sympathy from children who love them, making it seem disloyal of them to love the other parent:

> *Don't you leave me too… You're all I've got. Every time I see you hug him it's like someone stabbed me… We're all right together aren't we? We don't need him.*

Non-resident parents are in a weak position compared with the parents children live with. A lot of them are sufficiently intimidated by this kind of behaviour that the alienation actually works; the relationships between parents and children shrivel and visits gradually stop.

Father of girl now aged 8, and boy now aged 6

> *At the time I just couldn't stand it. Going down every Saturday – three trains and £30-odd quid – and then finding that the kids weren't there – or she said they weren't – or they were there but she made such a performance about where I was taking them that she really made it sound like I was going to kidnap them. Once they were crying and saying they didn't want to come with me she'd get all reasonable and say 'it's only daddy. I'm sure he'll take you on a nice walk' but it was too late then. The last time she actually said 'I'm so sorry, Marty' (all posh-like) 'I'm doing my best but it's not my fault they don't love you any more'. She's lucky I didn't slap her.*
>
> *I wish now I'd gone on somehow. Maybe I should have gone back to the solicitor. But that cost a bomb and anyway I was – how to put it? – offended. These are my kids and she shamed me with them and now it's almost two years since I saw them and it's too late.*

False Allegations

When a non-resident parent will not be put off but is insistent on seeing the children, and especially if both parents have been through mediation or the non-resident parent does go and seek advice from a solicitor, the resident parent may realise that she cannot continue refusing to let the children see their father without a very good reason and may set about producing one. She may go to CAFCASS or to a solicitor saying that there has been sexual abuse or domestic violence, or that there is some other reason to think that the child might be at risk. It may be suggested that the non-resident parent's environment would be unsafe or a bad influence (alcoholism, drug addiction and mental illness may be mentioned) or that, given the opportunity, the other parent will take the child away, possibly out of the country.

Such claims may or may not be accurate, but because they are about child protection (the court's principal concern) they will have to be investigated and legal aid will be provided. Even if the children are not old enough to understand what one parent is saying about the other, putting forward such accusations almost always has an alienating effect even if the accusations are without foundation, and a part of a deliberate attempt to discredit the father who totally denies them. In the meantime, once he has been accused he cannot continue to insist on seeing the children – and certainly must not attempt to do so without the mother's knowledge or against her wishes. Instead he will have to apply to the court for a contact order (see Chapter 4.5). The date for hearing such an order may be set months ahead, which, unless he is successful in getting an immediate interim contact order with the help of CAFCASS or a solicitor, could mean that the child does not see him at all during that period and as a result their relationship is further damaged.

Sometimes the claims a resident parent makes against the other parent strikes him or her as entirely outrageous. If they are produced out of the blue, having never been mentioned during preceding months of legal wrangling, it may be difficult to understand why anyone takes any notice. However, if there is the least chance that a parent has been abusive they cannot be allowed contact with the child until the matter has been investigated. On the other hand, the court recognises the importance to children of contact with both parents and must try to balance the two. Supervised contact, at a contact centre (see Chapter 4.5) or at the home of an approved relative, is often the court's best available compromise. However insulting it may feel to the parent, and however inadequate to the children's needs, it is better than no contact at all and it is usually assumed to be temporary. If all goes well the non-resident parent can apply after a few months to have contact liberalised.

Sometimes one parent's efforts to alienate children from the other parent are more than a reaction to immediate anger or hurt and a desire to protect the children, but are intentionally harmful: a weapon wielded by a vengeful ex-partner in an on-going adult war and intended not only to reduce a child's contact with the absent parent but also to damage that parent in every aspect of adult life. In the example below there had been escalating quarrels within the marriage and when it disintegrated both sought to be the resident parent, each claiming that the other was unfit:

> Michael alleged that Lizbeth was a problem drinker and that it was when she was drunk that their fights escalated. Lizbeth denied getting drunk although she did admit to heavier drinking due to the stress of marriage problems and Michael's anger.

> Lizbeth alleged that Michael pushed her on several occasions and maintained that the children saw the fighting on at least one occasion. She further alleged that Michael once threw a teapot at her, after which she called the police. It was this incident that led to the separation and to Lizbeth going to court to ask for residence and contact orders.

> Michael denied the domestic violence. He maintained that far from throwing the teapot at Lizbeth, he was trying to restrain her and in doing so the teapot was knocked off the table.

> Since the separation, the children have lived with their mother and been allowed only daytime visits with their father. When he applied to the court to amend contact, Lizbeth stated that the children were traumatised by the incident involving the teapot and the police and were frightened of Michael's anger.

> In addition, warned by her solicitor that she did not have the sympathy of the family court judge, Lizbeth put in a new statement telling the court that she is concerned that Michael cannot be trusted to maintain appropriate sexual boundaries with the children.

> Michael alleges that Lizbeth is attempting to alienate the children from him by exaggerating the violence and denying her contribution to it, and now by planning to accuse him of sexual abuse of the children.

Whether the final step in the escalating accusations was factually true or not, that angry couple had trapped their children in a double bind of damage. If a child is sexually abused by a parent the psychological damage can last a lifetime. But if a child who has not been abused is falsely led to believe that a loving parent harmed him or her, that distortion of reality can itself cause long-lasting psychological harm.

This is why allegations of parent incest trump all other weapons in alienation wars. When a parent makes that accusation to a mediator, social worker, solicitor or in court, it is clear that the child needs protection but it is not clear if the immediate need is for protection from the alleged offender or protection from false information by the accusing parent. The court must investigate the allegations and decide if they are true or not, but until all the evidence is weighed a balance ought to be struck that does not favour one parent over another. Unfortunately, because priority is usually given to protecting the child from abuse, courts often order that the child have no contact with the allegedly abusive parent until a comprehensive evaluation of the family dynamics has been made by experts and utilised by the court to make a determination.

Whatever the truth of the original accusation or the eventual outcome of proceedings, sexual abuse allegations ruin lives. Not only the lives of men (and occasionally women) whose ex-partners have accused them of abusing their mutual children, but also the lives of the children whose relationships with the accused parent will never recover. An allegation of sexual abuse can be dismissed as groundless, found unproven, even withdrawn, but it cannot be unmade. Men, even some whose ex-wives never really believed their own accusations but made them so as to keep access to a minimum, have lost jobs and friends as well as their children.

Mother of two girls aged 6 and 9

> " It wasn't really my fault. I didn't say he had, I only said he might. Anyway I didn't actually mean it. I just didn't want him taking my girls away from me every weekend. Somehow it got around, though, and the children were interviewed and the school knew and then I absolutely tried to stop it but I couldn't. In the end Eric was pushed out of his job – he was manager of a local supermarket – and his new woman walked out on him and he can't pay what he's meant to in maintenance. "

Protecting children's attachments while allegations against parents are investigated

In California and Florida attorneys and the courts have crafted plans so that when an accusation of sexual abuse is made by a parent the identified child continues to have a relationship with both parents, while being protected from harm caused by either of them. The success of these unique plans rests on the ability of the legal professionals to find an agreeable alternative living situation that will not be traumatic for the child as the investigation proceeds. One such plan involves a neutral adult (such as a friend of the family or family member) known to have a positive relationship with the child who is awarded temporary legal care of him or her. The designated adult may move into the family home and the parents temporarily move into another residence, or the child may move into the temporary caretaker's home. Frequent contact (often daily) with the child is awarded to the mother and father and may be supervised by the child's temporary legal guardian.

Another proposed plan involves a neutral family friend or member temporarily relocating to the state of legal jurisdiction for the divorce and then renting an apartment in which he or she will live with the child. Temporary guardianship is awarded to this adult who may act in the role of supervisor when the child has frequent scheduled visits with his or her parents.

These unique arrangements allow the child to maintain attachment relationships with both the mother and father while being protected both from potential sexual abuse by one parent and from destruction of a healthy attachment by the false accusations of the other. Although critics might question the appropriateness of the child being temporarily separated from both parents, a commonplace alternative (and the usual measure in the UK) is removal of the child into foster care with strangers. These arrangements are certainly a less traumatising way of accomplishing the essential protection of the child from potential sexual and psychological abuse and altered memories, as well as providing sufficient time for a careful and thorough investigation.

Sexton, McIntosh and Dickler, 2012

6.4 Avoiding alienation when agreement seems impossible

If you are really convinced that it is important to your children to have the best possible relationship with both parents, and you are therefore really determined to avoid alienating them from the other parent – let's say the mother – you can do it, even if there is no room for agreement or even politeness between you. There are arrangements that will ensure that your child can have contact with her without risk, and there are people and organisations who can help you to make them.

When one parent thinks the other is unfit

If you genuinely believe that your ex-partner is unfit to take sole charge of the children you will obviously try to make sure that doesn't happen. Making allegations of abuse, addiction or dangerous neglect may seem the easiest way but quite apart from their immorality, inaccurate or wildly exaggerated accusations may damage rather than protect the children. If you avoid alienating the children from her, even a mother who cannot take care of them on her own may still be able to have a loving relationship with them, and while their safety and wellbeing is of course your first priority, the best possible relationship with the other parent comes close behind.

How easy or difficult it is to make arrangements that meet both those demands mostly depends on your own relationship with the other parent. If she recognises her own shortcomings as a parent in sole charge, is as anxious as you are about the children's safety and is grateful to you for encouraging her contact with them, you may be able to make arrangements between you. That may sound like a very big 'if' but it does sometimes happen:

Father of boy aged 7 and girl aged 5

At the moment she's in rehab. She's an addict to just about any mind-altering stuff you can think of. She seems to get hooked on whatever's available and some of the mixtures she's taken in the last couple of years have been really dangerous. Last time I was away for work there was a fire. She didn't even wake but the kids got her out. Six and four they were then. That was it for pretending she was in charge of them. Luckily she knows. She loves them and she knows she can't be sure to keep them safe so she hasn't fought me. The kids see her at weekend visiting and when she comes out she'll probably come and see them here or come the summer they could go to the park with friends. She can't mother them but she's still their mother.

Mother of two girls aged 6 and 8

I divorced him when they were only three and one years old so I guess I could have sort of dropped him out of their lives. He was an alcoholic and family life just wasn't possible but he was – and is – a nice man and he loved them and still does, so I didn't want to take all that away. He sees them every week and always has. I wouldn't let them go away and stay with him because he mightn't be responsible, but he knows that himself and wouldn't ask. But they're perfectly safe going out with him in the daytime. They're movie-buffs, all three of them.

Of course most parents are not so accepting of being judged 'unfit' and many are extremely reluctant to abide by any restrictions that their ex-partners try to impose on their contact with the children, especially if there is no objective evidence against them, such as a relevant medical condition, criminal record, police warning or referral to social services. The most frequent focus for anxiety is overnight visits (see Chapter 7.3) and it is these which many parents – like the two quoted above – seek to prevent. Sometimes the resident parent's long and intimate knowledge of the other parent is enough to worry him or her. For instance, if a father has been irritable and not at all child-centred during the marriage, the mother may know that he will have no idea how to cope with the child's evening and bedtime routine and that he might lose his temper with the child if things went wrong. Sometimes, though, a father simply finds the prospect of the child being out of his care overnight intolerable, so every aspect of the mother's potential care strikes him as unacceptable. He may raise the spectre of neglect over trivial matters – such as the mother's habit of watching TV with the volume so high that he fears she might not hear the child if he woke – as well as over truly dangerous possibilities such as leaving the sleeping child alone in the house.

If you are generally managing polite if not mutual parenting, you may be able to talk through and resolve anxieties and arrive at mutually acceptable living arrangements for the children and visiting plans for the non-resident parent. However, you may find yourselves caught up in a vicious circle where anger and humiliation at not being trusted with his own child builds up to a point where the father breaks the agreed arrangements and so confirms his ex's suspicions about his untrustworthiness. The breaches may be trivial – bringing the child back a few minutes late, perhaps, or buying him a forbidden snack – but sometimes they are more serious.

If it proves impossible for both of you to honour shared arrangements you may need the help of the court in imposing them (see Chapter 4.5).

When one parent has been shown to be unfit

If your ex was physically abusive to one of the children, or to you – perhaps in sight of the children – or has been shown to have sexually abused one of the children, or if he has been convicted of some other appalling crime, it's entirely understandable if you do not want him to have anything further to do with you or the children. But if your desire to airbrush him right out of all your

Mother of girl aged 3

" *We agreed that he could take her to spend Saturday with his mother. The second time he did it he rang me to say they'd missed the train and would have to stay over. It was just an excuse. He did it on purpose. I just can't trust him to stick to what we've worked out.* "

lives and what is left of your family is understandable from your point of view, it is not desirable from your children's. Hopefully, when your fury and disgust at his behaviour begins to let up, you will see that you can't, and shouldn't, get rid of him altogether and that the law won't let you.

First the 'can't'. Whatever this man has done, he exists. However much you wish it weren't so, he is your children's biological father. To wipe him out you'd have to be prepared to tell whopping lies to the children when eventually they ask about their dad and to your family and friends and neighbours too. If he left and you remarried when the children were tiny you might pretend your second husband, their stepfather, is their father. If the children were old enough when he left to remember their father, you might tell them he is dead. But quite apart from the rights and wrongs of lying, you would certainly get caught out eventually and that would be the end of trust in your family.

Now the 'shouldn't'. All children – all people – have a deep-seated need to know about their parents and where they came from. You only have to look on the internet to see that huge numbers of adults spend hours trying to trace their lost beginnings. Most people accept that need in adopted or looked-after children and nowadays we take the trouble to be open with them so that they can ask questions when they're ready and deal with truthful answers even if they're painful. That need is exactly the same for children like yours whose fathers are absent because they abused them or you.

No parent should try to airbrush the other parent out of children's lives, even if they have been abusive, but that doesn't mean that an abusive parent should be invited in. If you are genuinely afraid of your ex you have every right to refuse to see him and the Family Court system will support you. But if he goes to the court asking to be allowed contact with the children, the court will not automatically refuse it because of what he did in the past, because being a father is not conditional on good behaviour and children have a right to the best possible relationship with both parents.

The court will call experts to explore the father's motives for seeking contact (does he really love the children or is he trying to use them to maintain power over you?). Those experts will seek to understand what happened in your ex's childhood that contributed to his crimes, and to assess the dynamics of his present family. A good court assessment can go a long way explaining what might have gone wrong in the parental relationship and to helping work out if a father should see the children or have any contact with them. Those assessments will also help to establish how the children really feel about their dad. Research shows that children are often so desperate not to hurt the parent they live with that they will say what they know she wants to hear rather what they actually feel. That can mean that yours say bad things about their father, and say they don't want any contact with him when, truthfully, like it or not, they love him.

After an expert assessment the court will decide whether your ex should be allowed to have contact with the children and if so, what kind and how much. You might find yourself ordered to allow him to see them regularly on his own; to have regular supervised visits with them in an approved place such as a contact centre; not to see them but to talk to them on the phone or by email and to write to them; or to have no direct contact with them but to send letters, birthday cards and perhaps presents via a solicitor.

The judgement the court makes may not be one that either you or your ex would have chosen, allowing him less contact than he asked for but more than you want him to have. However, if a full assessment has been carried out the expert report on which the court's decision is based will get it right for the children, and that is what matters most.

7 Sharing parenting

When spouses separate they stop being a couple but they don't stop being parents. Irrespective of who left whom or why, neither father nor mother is any less a parent than before the break-up. It took two of you to make your babies and neither of you could ever stop being their parent even if you wanted to. The importance to children of contact with both their parents during and after family breakdown cannot be overstated, and in the last ten years has been increasingly widely recognised in family law (see Chapters 4.5, 6.3 and 6.4). Indeed, legal recognition of parents' equality is mandatory in the USA, Australia and the UK. But if it is now generally accepted that mothers and fathers are equally parents, it is not generally agreed what being a parent means: the role that follows the fact. If you are equally parents does that automatically mean that your parenting is equal, and if so is that equality a matter of quality, quantity or both? In Australia mandatory legal recognition of the equality of separating parents was widely interpreted to mean both: fathers were to be viewed and dealt with in the courts as equally important as mothers and to have equal rights of access to the children. In the US – and now in the UK – the emphasis is on quality rather than quantity and on children's rather than parents' rights. Fathers' equal importance is more a matter of being equally as concerned for the children as the mother and equally responsible for ensuring their wellbeing than a matter of spending equal time with them.

A couple applying for a divorce must say which parent the children are to live with (the 'resident parent' or 'parent with care'), how access for the non-resident or 'contact parent' will be arranged, and who will pay what for the children's maintenance (see Chapters 4.4 and 4.5). It is usually accepted that most children will live more with one parent than the other (school makes that almost inevitable for over-fives), and that the parent the child mostly lives with will be the resident parent. They will be the one who can claim any child benefit and associated tax benefits, and to whom child maintenance must be paid.

But those answers to the court's questions are largely legal formalities. The practicalities of sharing parenting may be a different matter because provided separating parents are in agreement with each other and submit a joint, uncontested plan, they can make whatever actual arrangements they please. Nobody else cares whether the children really are spending more time with the 'resident parent' than the other, and of course there is nothing to stop parents sharing benefits or arranging maintenance between them. So the two of you have the freedom and the responsibility to answer those crucial questions: where and with whom are your children going to live? When and how is the other parent to see them? The questions are easier to ask than to answer. Arranging what you will hear solicitors or social workers call 'contact' or 'access' for the parent the children don't actually live with is both one of the most important and most difficult parts of post-separation life.

7.1 Towards child-centredness

From King Solomon-like solutions to child-centred parenting plans

Everyone surely has to accept that mothers and fathers are equally *parents*; it is a biological fact after all. But equal, or shared, *parenting* is a different matter that is widely misunderstood to mean that a mother and father ought to have as near half-shares of their children as is practically possible. Sometimes half-shares mean literally half of the children, cutting a family of siblings in two with one or more children going with mum and another with dad. More often it means half of each child, cutting children's time and lifestyle down the middle so that they spend roughly half their time with one parent and half with the other. None of that is quite as horrible as King Solomon's suggestion that the baby over whom two women were quarrelling should be cut in two so they could have half each, but where his suggestion was impossible (which is why it brought the women to their senses) these modern versions unfortunately are not, and once they are in place they often have their own inertia so that parents don't feel the need to think again. So think carefully before you embark on trying to make a fair division of your children, or of one child's time and presence, between the two of you. If you stand back a little you will see that if you do this you are treating them as if they are commodities, marital property to be shared like the furniture or the money in that joint account. Such an approach to sharing parenting is never the best and is often the worst and seriously damaging to children whose lives are salami-sliced.

All over the Western world there are babies, toddlers, schoolchildren and adolescents who are uprooted at more or less regular and frequent intervals from one parent's home and moved to the other's. They may never be sure which is home for them. There are 'access arrangements' that change children over mid-week so that they spend Sunday night to Wednesday afternoon in one household, Wednesday night to Sunday afternoon in the other. Some children spend alternate whole weeks with each parent and some alternate school terms. Probably the most common arrangement is for children to spend weekdays with one parent and weekends or alternate weekends with the other. This last arrangement is popular with adults because if the weekend is Friday afternoon to Monday morning it gives parents almost 'fair shares' of the children and that division often fits with patterns of children's school and the non-resident parent's working hours. It may or may not be popular with children. In some (usually well-to-do) communities, living and working in one place (usually thought of as home) and retreating to another holiday place for weekends is not unusual. If it makes a life-pattern that a child settles into and eventually enjoys, this plan may work well for the whole family. Don't take it for granted, though. As with every other aspect of coping with family breakdown better, you need to think about your own individual children.

Boy aged 10

> *All my school sports things are on Saturday and now I'm in year 5 I'm in the teams. Football now; cricket in the summer. When they said about going to my dad at weekends I did try to say about it but they didn't really take much notice. Dad said he'd drive me to school on Saturdays but we only did it once 'cause he said it was too far. I asked mum if I could just go to dad's on Saturday afternoon after the matches are over but she said that wouldn't be fair, as dad would only have me for one night. I think this way is not very fair on me.*

Girl aged 12

> *Mum gets all the homework hassles and washing uniform and driving to after-school stuff. We don't ever get to see each other in the daytime 'cause I'm at school, and we don't get to go out or have much fun time together in the evenings because it's always school again the next day. Sometimes I wish I could be with my dad when it's maths homework and be with my mum for a Saturday's shopping.*

Even when routine week-by-week arrangements are comfortable for children as well as adults, King Solomon often reappears on high days and holidays. Many children must eat two Christmas dinners, often one on the day and the other on Boxing day, and can only have school friends to their birthday parties every other year because on the alternate years it's the other parent's turn and the birthday celebration is too far away for school friends to join in. Dividing up these special days is very difficult (maybe heartbreaking would be a better word) and very individual, but it matters to children and can be done better. There are some suggestions from parents in Chapter 9.

A King Solomon approach to sharing parenting works for many mothers and fathers and because they tend to be overwhelmed with the adult aspects of their separation most of those do not even take the time to wonder if it's the best possible arrangement for their child or children. The non-resident parent – nine out of ten times, the father – often wants his 'fair share' of the children at almost any cost. He may feel, and advisers from his mother to his solicitor may tell him, that it's his right. Some fathers involved in arguments over arrangements for the children even feel that settling for less than the nearest possible to a fifty–fifty division of their time and presence might make his ex or the children themselves feel that he didn't care about them. The resident – and now single – parent, the mother, would often prefer the children to live with her full-time but usually acknowledges – or is forced by her solicitor to acknowledge – the 'justice' of their father's case. Sometimes, though, a mother may be far from reluctant for the children to spend time with their father. She may feel that it is only fair to her that her ex shares the childcare burden, giving her predictable stretches of child-free time and the opportunity to get a new life going.

Her ex

It's OK. He comes. His days are in my diary for the rest of term. His mother and I don't have to meet or discuss it. It's not perfect though, a bit rigid already and that'll get worse when he's older. Already it's tricky keeping to it in the holidays when he wants to have particular kids over and he's in the wrong place. It would work better if we lived even closer together. Special celebration days are tricky too. Does he just spend his birthday with whichever parent he happens to be with on the day it falls? And Christmas – well we've already had one of those and it was miserable.

Mother on half-week care arrangement

It works for me because I know exactly when he'll be with me and when I can have time off from mothering without having to pay a babysitter.

Their son aged 8

I'd just like to live somewhere and visit the other place. Other kids go home; I go to my dad's or to my mum's.

Wanting more, and less, of children's presence and direct responsibility for their care is understandable, but scenarios like those opposite can never be acceptable because they do not accommodate children's feelings and choices. Children need to meet family breakdown as their own people rather than their parents' treats or burdens.

Each of your children's lives belongs to him or her, not to either or both of you. It is the break-up of your marriage or other adult partnership that has made it necessary to formalise parenting into something shared between the two of you individuals rather than enjoyed by you both as a couple, and in this situation it is your child's rights that are in question rather than yours. It is every child's right to maintain the best possible relationship with each parent and it is your joint responsibility to facilitate that as best you can. As equal parents you each have one and only one right to a child: the right to opportunities to maintain a loving, caring relationship with them. That means, of course, that neither of you is entitled to try to belittle the other parent in your child's eyes (see Chapter 6) or to sabotage their communication or prevent them seeing each other, unless there is evidence that contact is unsafe.

7.2 Parenting plans

Parents, children and parenting plans are individual so no outsider – or even paid adviser – can tell you exactly what you should arrange. However, in the light of recent research, there are some basic recommendations and pitfalls that really do seem to apply to parents and children in general: parents in civil partnerships or same-sex marriages as well as heterosexual married couples or committed partners, and adopted as well as biological children from infants to students. Most of them have been discussed in detail in earlier chapters but the ones that are most important to your immediate decision-making are summarised here.

- Children's current and future happiness and wellbeing should be central to whatever parenting plans you make. Understandably a parent sometimes demands to know why: 'Why should children have priority? What about my happiness? Doesn't that matter just as much?' Of course the happiness of both parents matters – indeed it is probably a search for some kind of happiness for at least one of you that led to the breakdown of your family – but where your happiness and your children's happiness are at odds, children's must come first because while you are already formed adults, their lifelong development and their adult personalities, achievements and relationships depend on their emotional wellbeing through childhood. Having their family disintegrate and their parents living apart will in itself make children anxious and unhappy, of course, which is why it's not something any loving parent undertakes lightly. But by understanding which aspects of the new situation are most upsetting for this particular child at this particular time, and working to avoid or modify those even if you have to do so at your own expense, you can do a great deal to soften the impact (see Chapters 2 and 4).

- For many children the most important aspect of their parents' separation is not the obvious one – a parent moving out of the home to live elsewhere – but their mother and father's on-going relationship, or lack of it. In fact, most children are more upset by the hateful atmosphere and endless arguments (or worse) that surround family breakdown than they are by the separation itself. The least traumatic parental separation for children is one in which the mother and father can remain respectful of each other as joint parents even though they reject each other as partners (see Chapter 5 and Chapter 6.1). The most destructive separation is one where the couple's relationship becomes so toxic that one or both parents try to put the children off the other one and to persuade them to take sides (see Chapter 6).

- Even if neither parent deliberately tries to alienate the children from the other, either or both may be so overwhelmed with anger and jealousy, guilt and self-loathing that even when they are physically with their children they are emotionally absent. That kind of absence is as damaging as the physical kind. Preserving space for children in heads and hearts, desperately difficult though it may sometimes be, is the bedrock of their continued wellbeing which is why 'mutual parenting' (see Chapter 5.1) is the *ideal* to strive for. If both parents can manage to keep that space for their children, emotionally and practically, they may grow up unscathed (though not unchanged) by the separation.

- However mutual the parenting you are struggling towards there will certainly be upsets, especially at the beginning of life apart. When you are trying to get your toddler to bed and he's mixing hitting out at you with clinging to you, it's desperately depressing to realise that he's missing daddy's bedtime routine and stories and that yours aren't a satisfactory substitute. And when it's Friday night and you've made the especially nice supper tradition demands, but the older children turn sulky and unhelpful, it's demoralising to realise that a special Friday night supper was a family

Mother of three boys aged 2, 7 and 11

" *I think one of the worst things was realising that even when I was trying my hardest to give them as good a life as they'd had before, it wasn't good enough because their father wasn't there. I wasn't good enough because I'm not him.* "

tradition and they're missing the family part although you've
provided the traditional meal.

There will probably be many times like these when however
hard you are both trying to be supportive of each other as
parents, it's impossible not to be angry and/or guilty on your
children's behalf. You can see that they are suffering from
the breakdown of their family and you know that the two
of you brought it upon them. In the long-term, though, rage
and remorse for what's past won't help as much as thinking
positively about the future. When the current storms die down
your separation need not prevent your children from being
happy. Many children in so-called 'intact' families grow up and
flourish while one parent works away from home for substantial
periods of time. There are even some children whose securely
married parents choose to occupy separate homes and visit
each other. If there is a single, overwhelming difference
between those children and yours it is that their parents are
united though apart, and their children know it. You two are not
united (and your children know it) but mutual parenting can
come to mean that you are at one where they are concerned:
that you parent together although you're apart.

- Assessing and understanding children's happiness and
  wellbeing is crucial and must depend on their ages and
  stages of development and on careful observation of their
  behaviour (see Chapter 2). A teenager can and should be
  consulted about all plans that involve him and he may often
  be allowed to choose. A baby cannot choose and her
  contentment with arrangements can only be judged by
  concentrated attention to her behaviour and not being too
  ready to ascribe everything undesirable to teething. Between
  those extremes, a three-year-old's distress at the prospect of
  going to spend a weekend away from her mum, or a six-year-
  old's sudden anxiety about going to school, should certainly
  be heard and carefully thought about, but should not always
  be directly acted upon as immediate happiness and long-term
  wellbeing may not be the same (see Chapter 1).

- Often, though, immediate happiness and long-term wellbeing
  are the same and if your eight- or 11-year-old feels able to talk
  to you and is sure that you will hear, he may tell you what he is
  missing most, she may tell you what keeps making her cry and
  you may be able to put sticking plaster on the worst wounds.

- Parenting plans need to be regular and predictable enough that
  all concerned – adults as well as children – can rely on them
  and come to take them for granted instead of wasting time and
  energy planning (and arguing) week by week. If it is part of
  the agreement that you will drive the children to meet up with
  their father each Sunday (perhaps because the family car has

Father of girl aged 6

" *It was only the
'parenting plan' idea
that made Amelie's
mother think
seriously about the
possibility that she
might live with me
rather than her.* "

stayed with you) doing so must be a real commitment; and if father is due to visit at a particular time on a particular day, he must be there more or less on the dot, always.

- But within the regularity that will help children come to feel safe and secure in the new arrangements, there also needs to be some flexibility, both week by week and in the long-term, and this is yet another instance of mutual parenting scoring more highly than any alternative type. The fact that father routinely brings the toddler home to his mother at 7 p.m. on Sunday evenings should not mean that he cannot be brought home an hour earlier on one particular Sunday when his grandparents are to visit at 6 p.m. Only a desire to assert himself over the mother could make a father refuse to sacrifice that single hour to a visit that will be a treat for the child (and the grandparents). On another Sunday you may find yourself grumbling that 7 p.m. is not 7.10 p.m. – it isn't, of course, but the train may think that it is. Niggling insistence from either of you on the other parent sticking to the very letter of your arrangements will suggest that your parenting agreement has not been made willingly. It may need revision if it is to survive.

- In the long-term parents need to be prepared to change arrangements, even arrangements they themselves are comfortable with, in order to keep them comfortable for children. Children grow and change. Plans that suit a toddler may not suit him at all when he is four years old and starting school, while routines for a child newly at secondary school may need to change several times in her first year to accommodate her new independence and peer group (see Chapter 2).

Fathers & mothers

When you are making – and remaking – parenting plans, it's important to believe and hang on to the fact that mothers and fathers can share equally in everything that matters most about being a parent – concern, responsibility and reciprocated love for every child – without taking or vying for equal shares of their time.

Although more and more fathers in intact couples play a very big part in children's daily lives, few – less than 10% – become the resident parents of their children after family breakdown. There are all kinds of reasons and composites of reasons why this is so, ranging from unrealistic but still pervasive conventions about divisions of family labour (dad earns, mum cares) to down to earth practicalities about working hours and schools.

Fathers often press for more contact, and especially for overnight visits from children, not because they actually want that extra time right now but because they fear that they will otherwise lose (or fail to build) their close relationship with their children after the separation. Research strongly suggests that this particular fear is groundless. The quality of contact – parent and child looking forward to seeing each other and having fun together – is far more important than its quantity, and for all but the youngest children, frequent communication, in all available forms – Skype, email and text, as well as phone, letters and postcards – thickens up the parent–child relationship between physical meetings.

If the arrangements you make for your children's lives after family breakdown are to optimise their security and wellbeing, they must reflect or at least take account of their lives when you were together. Within many separating couples, involvement and concern (as well as love) for a child is mutual, but one parent is better able than the other to manifest that concern as practical caring. In the early years especially, the prior relationship between parent and child, and the extent to which it has been hands-on, is critical to future planning. Although the numbers of fathers taking an active part in their children's care is increasing rapidly, it is still the case that, irrespective of what either of them might have preferred, many more mothers than fathers have been children's principal caregivers since they were born.

Daytime-only contact does not reduce attachment

'[O]vernight care in early infancy does not appear to determine attachment security with the second parent. Warm, lively, attuned caregiving interactions between baby and the second parent appear to be central to the growth of attachment security in that relationship.'

McIntosh, 2011

Fathers in sole charge

Recent American research shows that:

- One third of fathers with working wives are a regular source of childcare for their children; this figure is higher in some non-white families.
- The number of dads regularly caring for their children increased from 26% in 2002 to 32% in 2010.
- Among fathers with pre-schoolers in 2010: 20% were primary caregivers.
- The number of 'stay-at-home dads' increased by 50% between 2003 and 2006.

American Psychological Association, 2013

Despite these hopeful statistics, there are still many men, including truly loving fathers, who have never changed that proverbial nappy and would be at a loss if left for more than half a day in sole charge of a baby or toddler. This is one of the better reasons why fewer fathers than mothers become the resident parent.

Even with older children, a father who has not played much part in the practical details of their lives while the family was intact may struggle to keep them safe, secure and happy if he is suddenly left to cope alone. If you do not know the name of your eight-year-old's best friend (this week) or teacher (this term)

Mother of boy aged 8 months

❝ I'd trust him absolutely to do what's necessary for Liam but I wouldn't trust him to do, or even to wonder, what's nice. ❞

you'll have to climb to the top of a very steep learning curve before she is likely to be happy with you picking her up from school.

Girl aged 7

> *I get muddled who's picking me up and where I'm going. My teacher tries to help. I think she has stuff about it written down. But I don't like it; don't like it that I don't know who to look for… that's why I was crying when he came yesterday. Not 'cause he was late or 'cause I didn't want to go with him like my mum said but 'cause I wasn't sure it was going to be him or who.*

You can learn, now, what you did not feel the need to know before, and children who love you will help. But the learning may take time. So both of you need to think honestly and realistically about what the sharing arrangements you are considering adopting immediately will actually be like for each of your children. Are they the arrangements that will best maximise each child's happiness in this unhappy situation, irrespective of your adult convenience, or are they the arrangements that best suit you two or that strike you as 'fair'?

Girl aged 12 with a sister aged 3

> *It was too far and cost too much for daddy to come to see us for the day so we had to go for weekends. Staying with him at the beginning was really sort of scary. He'd made a room for us which was OK-ish but no nightlight and he hadn't bought the kind of food Amelia ever eats (pork chops for supper and no biscuits) and he sort of didn't know how to look after her – or me come to that. He'd bathed Amelia and put her to bed lots of times and so he did that OK but then he came downstairs leaving her wide awake in a strange room and I had to take her for a wee and stay while she settled. Luckily I'd been allowed to babysit her sometimes since my birthday so she was used to me taking care of her at night. But in the morning she was awake long before dad (and long before I usually get up at weekends) so I had to wake up too and help her find clothes and get dressed and everything and it just didn't feel like there was anybody but me in charge.*

Some fathers are not competent as carers when they are in sole charge of very young children but they are not the only ones. Some mothers are not competent either. It can't be taken for granted that being almost entirely with the mother as 'primary caregiver' will make a child happier now or be better for his attachment security and positive adjustment in the future. Being a lone parent is extraordinarily different from being a partnered one, and even mothers who feel that their ex played little part in the children's lives before the separation sometimes have trouble coping when they find themselves on their own. If such a mother also has a history of mental illness or depression, or if she is battling depression for the first time now, the stress of being left with almost unrelieved and solitary childcare may reduce the quality of her relationship with the child and the care she can give. Provided the father's motivation and intentions are good, he is emotionally and physically available to the child and her safety with him is not in question, having her spend time with him may be valuable to all concerned, even if his parenting is not conventionally competent.

Shared parenting usually means shared resources of which money and housing are the most immediately important (see Chapters 4.1 and 4.4). It's commonplace – even expected – for separating parents to quarrel over these but before you get involved, or let your solicitors get you embroiled, take time to think about how much these adult-sounding issues can affect your children. Any arrangement that leaves one of you much poorer than the other can seriously jeopardise the poorer parent's opportunities for a loving, caring relationship with the children, and can even deprive them of contact.

Either parent may end up on the losing side of a division of already-scarce resources. Mothers' financial situations often nosedive after separation because their ex-husbands cannot or will not pay anything approaching adequate maintenance (see Chapter 4.4) and their own earnings are inadequate or even threatened. Some women who continue to work full-time after separation nevertheless find it impossible to run what was a family home on their single earnings. And some women have to give up work once they are on their own because their hours, their earnings and the costs of childcare do not balance. Sudden household poverty can drain children's lives of accustomed pleasures. Even those who are old enough to understand that you are broke rather than mean are liable to resent your sudden refusal to let them go on school trips, carry on with out-of-school music or judo classes or dole out their accustomed pocket money.

Girl aged 9

" Half-term with daddy was kind of like camping. I slept on a mat and there was funny food and not much washing. It was really fun. "

Fathers, perhaps especially fathers who are trying hardest
to behave decently when their families break-up, are just as
likely to be left relatively poor and where housing is concerned
it is often fathers who suffer most. If the family was already
struggling to meet mortgage and utility payments, divorce
may be a final straw. If the whole ex-family has to move out
and find alternative living accommodation some (basic) kind of
housing will be provided for the mother and children but not
for the father. He has become a single man whose welfare is no
authority's responsibility and who may be left literally homeless.

If the separating couple is better off the father may move
out of the family home leaving the mother and children in it,
however, unless he is notably well-off, it may be difficult, even
impossible, to finance a second place to live where the children
can comfortably visit. A room may be the best such a father
can afford and even if he moves into a flat the chances of both
parental homes being equally child-friendly are very small.
If your new 'home' is notably less nice than the family home
you have left, your ex – or you yourself – may feel that it is not
suitable for a baby or safe for a toddler, while older children will
inevitably regret, even resent moving between the two places
however eager they are to spend time with both people. If a child
visits reluctantly, his time with you will do little to build your
relationship and may actually make it more difficult to maintain.

Father of boy aged 6

*I wanted equal time as a parent and my ex went along
with it because it meant she was only a single mother
part-time. But the truth is that by the time I'd paid rent
for the flat and maintenance to her for the kid, I was too
broke to give Eric a great time. I couldn't afford lots of
trips and days out; the flat was cramped, there wasn't
a garden and he didn't have any friends nearby. I knew
he'd rather be at home with his mum and his mates and
who could blame him?*

However mutual your parenting, you cannot stretch a tight
budget further than it can reach but you can resist scoring over
each other financially or listening to lawyers telling you what
you are entitled to instead of relying on your own sense of what
will make the best of a bad job. If you are both trying to support
each other's parenting so that the children can benefit from it, an
equal distribution of what's available is much more meaningfully
fair than equal shares of children's time.

Equal parenting and poverty

In the UK separation or
divorce is a commonplace
reason for employed men,
especially men over 50,
becoming homeless.

Ben Jackson, director
of communications
at Shelter, said 'last
year more than 27,000
householders became
homeless as a direct
result of relationship
breakdown'.

Warnes and Crane, 2004

7.3 Putting your parenting plan into action

Which of you is the resident parent and which the non-resident affects tax and benefit matters, but only affects your parenting plans if you cannot agree your roles and must therefore seek legal intervention. Provided you agree you can make whatever arrangements you please for the children. Unless the children are considered to be at risk, nobody is interested in whether or not they actually spend the stated alternate weekends and one night in the week with the non-resident parent.

The smooth running of contact between your children and their non-resident parent depends on both of you accepting your own and each other's different formal roles and both being firmly committed to continuing contact at all costs. The most helpful stance you, as resident parent, can adopt is as an active and proactive supporter of the relationship between each of your children and their mum or dad, not only practically but also in the emotional sense of expecting and encouraging children to enjoy it. Perhaps only someone who has seen their excited child off on an expedition with the other parent, so eager for the 'hello hug' that she forgets a goodbye one, can understand how difficult that can be. But given that you could not all stay contentedly together as a family, this is the very best you can do and in the long run of your child's development, worth any amount of effort. If your effort is to pay off, your ex also needs to be active and proactive over contact. Being active means taking a full part in planning and making arrangements for the children and then sticking to them – cheerfully. Being proactive means finding different ways of spending quality time with the children and being alert to any problems and eager to discuss them.

However hard you are each trying, though, minor difficulties with contact arrangements are inevitable, especially at the beginning. Whether you are the resident or the contact parent, you are human and under tremendous stress. You can forget things (that swimming gear, *again*) be late for pick up or drop off, seem grumpy or disapproving of the other parent or strain your parenting plan by allowing or encouraging a child to behave in ways the other parent has vetoed (too much TV). The great majority of contact problems are of this kind. They are the kinds of niggle that are normal within most intact marriages and, given mutual goodwill, easily overlooked or dealt with by compromise. It is when goodwill is lacking that difficulties escalate into conflicts that can threaten contact itself.

Mother of two boys aged 8 and 9

> " *I love my time with the kids. I get through the working week for those weekends with them. But I dread picking them up and taking them back 'cause it seems I can't do anything right. I try very hard not to be late but with the trains, it can happen, and you should hear him if I'm early… I try to do things with the boys that he'll approve of, like swimming, but last time we did that it turned out that Felix had had an ear infection and wasn't supposed to go in the water. He hadn't told me, had he? But that didn't stop him calling me irresponsible in front of them both. As for food: you'd never think I'd been the one who shopped and cooked for them for seven years. He quizzes me about what they've had so I feel I should be writing out menus. It can't really be that he doesn't trust me: I'm a good mum and always have been. So the truth is he doesn't want me to have them; maybe he hopes I'll drop out.* "

When contact is difficult to arrange so that children are often kept on tenterhooks and sometimes disappointed, or if visits are more or less miserable and children are reluctant, it's all too easy for one or both parents to decide that the children would be better off without it, or simply to let it dwindle and lapse. Easy, but wrong. A very large body of research says that there are no circumstances in which it is better for a child to lose touch with a parent after family breakdown or eventual divorce. There are many different types of contact. If one really cannot be made to work, try another.

Drifting away from contact with absent parents

In an American sample of more than 11,000 children, two thirds of separated fathers were consistently, over time, either highly or rarely involved with their children. However *almost a quarter of separated fathers started with frequent contact, which gradually dwindled to nothing.*

High levels of father involvement were more likely when children were older at the time of separation and were more likely to be maintained when fathers and mothers lived close to each other.

Separated mothers were more likely to be highly involved with their children and much less likely to drift out of contact.

Cheadle, Amato and King, 2010

Overnight contact – ages and circumstance

Most contact arrangements include overnight stays, often one or two weekend nights at a time and sometimes some half-term or holiday nights also. It is overnight contact that causes most problems both for parents and for children. When it works well there are major advantages over day visits, notably that the child has the opportunity to 'live with' the contact parent; that the two of them have a base rather than having to spend their time together visiting relatives or friends, making expeditions or wandering aimlessly around the park; and that the contact parent cares for the child through every minute and aspect of his or her way of being.

However, shared parenting that includes overnight stays may be impossible because of one parent's accommodation or lack of it, and even when it is practically possible it does not always work well from children's point of view. Separating couples need to face up honestly to the possibility that overnights will not work. Possible risk factors include a particular child being too young; one or the other household having inadequate income or housing; and one or the other parent being unable to provide appropriate care, having too long and too inflexible working hours or living at too great a distance.

Girl aged 4

Daddy wears glasses in the night and contact lenses in the day! I saw him put them in…

Special considerations in contact arrangements for infants (see Chapters 2.1 and 2.2)

- The impacts of parental conflict and violence – and their associated effect on parenting sensitivity – are especially damaging during the first four years of brain maturation.
- Extra care needs to be taken with the nature of separation from a primary attachment figure during the first two to three years. Well-managed, brief separations are indicated in the first two to three years, growing in duration through the fourth and fifth years.
- In early infancy, overnight stays are contra-indicated, undertaken only when necessary or helpful to the primary caregiver, and when the second parent is already an established source of comfort and security for the infant.
- Time spent with the second parent should enable maintenance of comfortable familiarity, and growing attachment security. Frequency of these visits should not create discontinuity or fragmentation for the young infant within their primary attachment relationship.
- The core consideration and determining factor is whether the proposed parenting plan and the method of its enactment will contribute to or detract from the emotional security of the infant.

McIntosh, 2011

Sleepovers for babies and toddlers

Staying overnight with the contact parent does not only mean that the child has to go to and settle in an unaccustomed place but also, of course, that he must leave the resident parent and the home set-up in order to do so. The younger the child the more likely it is that the leaving element – leaving mum and home – will be stressful. As suggested earlier, overnight stays for babies and toddlers should not be taken for granted (see Chapter 1). They may work well for all concerned if the parents were equal carers while the family was intact and the child is equally attached to both, and they may be helpful overall if the resident parent badly needs respite, but generally speaking regular and frequent nights away should usually be delayed until a child is three or four years old.

Outcomes of overnight contact for babies & toddlers

'Regardless of socio-economic background, parenting or inter-parental cooperation, babies under 2 years who spent one or more overnights a week with the second parent showed a cluster of stress regulation problems … Older infants, aged 2–3 years, who spent 2–3 nights per week with the second parent, also showed greater problematic behaviours than children in lower frequency overnight care, including heightened separation distress, aggression, eating problems and poor persistence.

These findings are consistent with the only other study of infants in overnight care, conducted by Solomon and George, who found a greater propensity for anxious, unsettled behaviour in infants when reunited with the primary caregiver, and greater propensity for development of insecure and disorganized attachment with the primary caregiver.'

McIntosh, 2011

If you do decide to include overnight stays with the non-resident parent in your parenting plan for a baby or toddler, it may be quite difficult to be sure how these are affecting him. You and his father will both need to put yourself in his small shoes in order to understand. A one- or two-year-old who is going for an overnight stay is not old enough to understand the plan or to anticipate how long he will be away, so although he may well be distressed at the point of separation from you he'll be no more distressed than if he was going to dad for the afternoon. Once that mini-parting is over he is misleadingly likely to appear to 'settle' with his father in the new place and it is only when he is returned home and reunited with you that the full extent of any upset will become clear. It is *the mother's relationship* with the child that is vulnerable to too-early separations and you are the one who will bear the brunt of his clingy and unsettled behaviour.

The fact that your baby or toddler seems happily settled while he is away with his dad and very obviously unsettled when he comes back to you may easily mislead you both. Your ex, understandably, may feel that he is doing fine because the baby was happy with him and the overnight was stress-free. Something you did must have caused the child's unusual behaviour when it was over. You, equally understandably, may feel that the baby's father is to blame – perhaps for letting him stay up too late or watch too much TV – and you may resent the fact that stress-free visits for him always mean a stressful couple of days for you.

The research information noted in the box above was gathered for very large groups of children from many different families. It does not mean that staying with dad overnight should be ruled out for your particular baby or toddler, or that it will certainly be appropriate for your individual four-year-old. You, your children and your environments are all unique. The mix of your relationships, your ex's relationships, temperaments, needs and circumstances may be a recipe that makes any contact arrangement stressful for the child or makes it supportive. What the research information does mean is that if you are making contact arrangements for a baby, toddler or preschool child, you need to consider questions such as the following very carefully before you settle on frequent overnight stays:

- What is the child's existing relationship with her father? Leaving you in order to stay with daddy overnight is unlikely to be upsetting if he was her primary or equal caregiver before the separation, or he is entirely accustomed to caring for her and she demonstrates her attachment to him by readily turning to him when she needs reassurance or comfort. However, if hands-on parenting of this child will be more or less new to them both, overnights with the father should ideally wait until some months of daytime contact have helped them to build a relationship.
- Can her father provide constant personal care while the child is with him? If he will need to go out to work or to socialise and plans to employ a babysitter, he is not in a position to have such a young child to stay with him. However, if the child has a caregiver at home, a nanny, au pair or babysitter,

having that person go with her to the father's home overnight may solve that problem as well as giving him some support in caring for her.

- Are there older siblings who will regularly and frequently stay overnight with their father? If so it may be difficult to arrange separate daytime contact for the youngest child and seem better for everyone if all the children go together (see Chapter 3.1).
- The more frequent and the longer overnight stays are, the more stress they tend to put on a child. Consider one night at a time rather than two, and on alternate weekends rather than every week, with daytime contact in between.
- Do you have urgent practical reasons for wanting this child to be away from home overnight? If you have mental or physical health problems or are suffering from stress or exhaustion, overnight breaks can help you to maintain the quality of your parenting. However, if separating from you to stay with her father is, in the event, unmanageably stressful for the child, any respite her absence might give you will be lost because it is on her return home and in her relationship with you that her anxious, unsettled, clingy or aggressive behaviour will show itself.
- These changes in behaviour may reflect real and lasting disturbance to a child's development rather than a temporary 'upset'. It is enormously important that even the youngest child sees the contact parent regularly, but how that is arranged is equally important.

Overnight visits for older children

Although it would be idiotic to suggest that a child under four is better off without overnight contact but becomes ready for it on his fourth birthday, these research studies do strongly suggest that staying away overnight becomes less difficult at around that age.

Overnight contact for 4 & 5-year-olds

'For 4- to 5 year-olds with separated parents, high inter-parental conflict and low parental warmth independently predicted a number of emotional regulation problems in children. Overnight time arrangements did not predict outcomes in this age group.'

McIntosh, 2011

School-aged children are far less likely to find leaving you for a night or two highly stressful in itself. Their attachment is developed, and hopefully secure, and their ability to understand plans and anticipate reunion is dawning if not yet complete. Furthermore, many of them are becoming accustomed to sleepovers with friends, which means not only that they are accustomed to being away from you but also that they are used to sleeping in a different bed in another house. For these older children what matters most of all is that spending time with their father, and staying overnight with him, is a pleasure, in prospect and in fact. Of course this mostly depends on the relationship between them and on issues dealt with earlier such as whether or not the child will be with siblings and where and how the contact parent lives. However, there are other points that may be important to smooth-running contact that is satisfactory for the child however difficult it may be for one or both parents.

- Being not only allowed but also encouraged to look forward to the contact times. You can easily turn pleasurable anticipation into guilt by denigrating the father or bemoaning your loneliness when the child is away (see Chapter 6).
- Feeling able to talk to one parent about time spent with the other but never being pressured to do so or asked to carry messages between the two.
- Having arrangements with a balanced mixture of regularity and flexibility. A child will not look forward to a weekend with dad if she will be missing her best friend's birthday party.
- Having the contact parent's full-time attention. Arriving for the weekend to find that dad has to work on Saturday is a put-down, whatever care he has arranged to cover his absence. Equally, the child wants to spend time with his father not with his father's friends or his lover, so extra adults are usually unwelcome (see Chapter 3).
- Something fun to do with the parent. Overnight visits work best when the child gets to do something with dad that he really enjoys and doesn't otherwise get to do regularly.
- Being able to keep in contact with home life during contact visits. Children should be free to phone or text the other parent and to do so privately if they wish. For older children in particular, contact with friends is overwhelmingly important. A child who texts or goes on Facebook from home should not need special permission to do so when with the other parent, and a spare phone-charger to keep there and perhaps the gift of an agreed number of extra minutes will help to prevent her from feeling cut off (see Chapter 4).
- With school the next morning, Sunday evenings are often rushed and stressful even when children have been at home

Boy aged 9

It's since I started going to my dad's at weekends that I've really started swimming. We go to a great big pool and he comes in with me to swim and then I get a swimming lesson. Last week the teacher said I'm doing well and this week I'm moving up a group.

all weekend; having been away, combined with the transition from one parent to another, can make things worse. To keep Sundays calm, children need to feel comfortable fulfilling school commitments during weekend visits. There must be time, encouragement and a suitable place to do homework, revise for an exam or practise a musical instrument.

Teenagers often find regular weekend contact very difficult even if parents allow some flexibility. Both of you need to accept that:

- The young person's peer group probably matters more to her than either parent (at least at a conscious level). She wants to be where her friends will – or can – be. Unless the parents live in the same area, she is not likely to want to go away very often.
- Most young people are very bad at making plans in advance. Your teenager will not be able to choose which weekends he can be away without missing anything that matters to him because he will not know what he will be doing and when. It is useless to pressure him to decide because he has no idea what his friends will be doing when, either. The chances are that none of them will be doing anything adults recognise as special (and can therefore put in a diary). What they will be doing is hanging out.
- If the father's area or home offers something interesting (such as proximity to an important football stadium or a seaside location), encouraging the teenager to invite friends to come with her may help to keep up her enthusiasm for weekends with her father. She may not accept, though. However much her father has to offer, she may not want to mix friends from one home and parent with the other.
- The only thing that really matters about contact is that the child and her father spend enjoyable time together. If your teenager no longer enjoys regular weekends or even resents the pressure to go on with them, her father might offer to meet up with her for supper and a movie in her home area, or to rendezvous in the nearest town. Even if it is not taken up, any such suggestion will make it clear that dad is eager to see her on whatever terms she finds comfortable.

Handling handovers

Whether they are going out for an afternoon, a weekend or a week's holiday, most children – especially very young ones – find the actual transition from the care of one parent to the care of the other confusing and stressful. The more often such a transition is made (and the less well the parents manage it) the more disturbing the contact arrangement is.

- Make sure your child passes rapidly and seamlessly (or better still, with a couple of minutes of overlap) from your care to her father's (or via a third party if necessary). Even a moment when she's not sure which parent is in charge of her may be enough to make her panicky.
- If you and your ex can't manage to meet and be friendly, even for five minutes, don't put your child to wait for daddy alone at the front gate feeling that nobody's in charge of her. Use an intermediary instead; dropping her off with somebody she knows and likes from whose home daddy can collect her.
- She must be allowed to take special precious possessions backwards and forwards with her. A baby's special blanket or teddy is obvious, but her older brother's old-fashioned, illuminated and loudly ticking clock may be almost as important to him at bedtime.
- Make the changeover positive: she needs to be sure that you want her to go, her father wants her to come and you're both certain that she'll have a nice time.
- Keep the actual parting brief. Don't tell her *again* how much you'll miss her or revisit plans and arrangements that have already been discussed. 'I love you. See you tomorrow' is enough.

Daytime contact & geography

Seeing the contact parent during daytime rather than overnight visits suits a lot of children, especially the very young. If parents live close to each other and their parenting is at least polite if not mutual (see Chapter 5), daytime contact is so easy that overnight or weekend visiting that is genuinely for everyone's pleasure often develops out of it.

As the children quoted here grew older they began to choose which household they would be in on any particular day and by the time they left primary school they could (and often did) walk between the two homes. They had a bedroom as well as a parent in each.

From children's points of view that is an ideal to aspire to but it is not one that many couples will achieve because living close together with a lot of popping in and out going on is not what most people who are separating or divorcing want. Even if they don't want to see each other, though, parents who want the children to see both of them need to recognise that geography is crucial (see Chapter 4) because living close to one another is what will make that possible. What is more, children are more likely to feel that being with daddy is an integral part of their daily lives rather than something special and separate, if being with him at weekends begins with him driving them to their

> ## Swapping from the care of one parent to the other
>
> Further data from the study of overnight care (see p.138 and p.140) also identified that 'frequent transitions of care between parents who remain acrimonious and struggle to facilitate a smooth transition for the infant' as adding to the difficulties.
>
> McIntosh, 2011

Twin girl and boy aged 4

We like having sleepovers with our dad don't we, Tom? But you always have to go home in the middle of the night don't you? And then I have to go too.

Saturday activities, and he always does something with them on inset days or at half-term.

If the two of you live a long distance apart, visits will cost a lot of money – in fares or petrol – and time, and a few hours with the child may not be enough to make the journey seem worthwhile for him or the resultant freedom worthwhile for you. Furthermore, it is really difficult to have a good time with a child without a base to go to. Football in the park is fine while the sun shines and the child's energy runs high, but what if it pours with rain and he is tired? Under those circumstances 'ordinary' families go home and a young child will not fully understand why dad and he cannot. Whether you have decided to stick with daytime contact because your child is too young for sleeping away or because the father's accommodation isn't suitable for overnight stays, this is a fragile kind of contact, which all too often deteriorates and then fades away.

Mother of three children, separated for two years

> *I regret the contact now. I wish I'd broken it completely. I don't think he'd have bothered taking me to court if I'd said no. I thought the kids needed a link with him – and maybe they do – but their contact with him has been so erratic that they've never known if he was coming or not and that's probably been more damaging than if they'd just never seen him.*

Since nothing apart from losing both parents is more damaging to a child than having one parent vanish out of her life, it is worth considering some ways of making daytime contact with a parent who doesn't live nearby easier and more lasting:

- Could you, the resident parent, allow your ex to use yours and the child's own home as a base for visits? If you don't want to see your ex you could go out for the afternoon. If you can't bear the idea of him being in the house alone as if it was still his, would your mother or a friend agree to be there?
- If your home is completely out of bounds, is there a relative or friend whom you trust and the child knows and likes who would let them meet in her house?
- Does the child already spend occasional nights with grandparents or other relatives who live locally? If so, could father visit the child there?
- Is there an activity centre that your child enjoys to which you could drive her to meet and spend time with her father who would then bring her home?
- Failing anything more personal, is there a contact centre to which you could drive the child to meet up with her father?

For older children and teenagers daytime visits between weekends or holidays may be the more valuable because of the effort they cost the contact parent. They will know that if dad takes all that trouble to get to the school play or the GCSE subject choice evening or an important cricket match, he really cares about their lives.

Sometimes these visits can take place without the parents meeting each other: a school play often has two or three performances and parents could therefore go separately. A concert is a one-off, though, and so is a sports event or a school consultation so although attending such functions together may not be something you discussed when you were first making parenting plans, it is an issue that eventually needs to be addressed. Teenage or student accomplishments often involve public performance or acknowledgement. Is one of you always going to miss the days when your child most wants you to be proud of him – such as school prize giving or university graduation day? And what about the opposite kind of day when he needs a parent's presence and support: will only one of you answer a call from A&E or even the police station?

Supervised daytime visits

Sometimes a mother really does not want her children to see their father at all, even for brief daytime visits. Her ex cannot insist on seeing the children against her wishes but neither can she prevent him just because that is what she would prefer (see Chapter 6.3). Sometimes a father is so intimidated by an angry ex that he backs off and the children are deprived of contact with him.

If the two parents cannot sort the question of father's access out between them the matter should go to court where, although he may not realise it, the father can apply for a contact order (see Chapter 4.5). Once an application has been made parents are in the court's hands. It will make an order if it thinks that is in the child's best interests, but it may not be the order they expected or would have chosen. Child protection is the court's priority so the mother's concerns and accusations will be carefully listened to. However, the court is also concerned for the children's contact with both parents and will try to balance the two. The court's best available compromise is often weekly or fortnightly daytime visits that are supervised by an approved third party: sometimes a social worker at a contact centre, sometimes a grandparent or other relative at her home. Most mothers are indignant that any contact is being ordered against her expressed wishes; most fathers find compulsory supervision of their brief time with the children deeply insulting. But however inadequate such meetings may be, both to the children's needs and to their father's, they are better than no contact at all. The court sees supervised contact as temporary. When its enquiries have been completed, probably with the help of reports from expert witnesses, a contact order can be put in place.

Contact from a distance

In this era of increasingly sophisticated communications parents and children can stay in touch with each other even when they cannot spend time together and it's important to realise how much this can help their relationships, even when practical circumstances are against them. The point of regular and frequent contact with the non-resident parent is to assure children that although he is no longer physically present in their home, their father is still their father and as loving, interested and concerned for them as ever. And when children are with the father on holiday, they similarly need to know that although they are away from their mother she is still there for them. However desperately an absent parent misses being with a child in person – talking and listening, hugging and holding hands, playing games and washing faces – he can give this assurance in words and pictures – provided they are the right ones. Not all the right ones will be hi-tec. Most children love getting mail and will be thrilled with letters, provided they are typed so that a child who can read at all can read them privately rather than having them read to her and dad doesn't expect a long screed in return. Picture postcards are fun to get and keep – your child might like an album to collect them in – and sending one back requires only a few written words. A weekly card could show where daddy has been or something he's seen (OK, you're still in Manchester like last week, like always, but this is a different bus!), and you could give your child a supply of stamped addressed postcards to send back.

The phone is an obvious channel of communication but sometimes expensive – especially if you are on different continents – and not always very comfortable for children under about five. Younger ones may love to 'answer' the phone when it rings but often find it very difficult to listen to what the caller is saying and then reply. If your child is comfortable using a phone, you might consider giving him a pay-as-you-go mobile rather earlier than you would have done if the family had stayed intact, so that he knows he can call you to make arrangements or to chat, and do so privately. Some children find it difficult to talk in front of mum or in front of siblings. Older children are usually inseparable from their mobiles, which means that you can reach out to them at almost any time. Being phoned is disruptive, though. You obviously shouldn't phone your child during the school day and you won't want her trying to phone you when you are in a meeting. The solution is texting, and today's children become exceedingly competent at sending texts and at reading them at a surprisingly early age. If by any chance you haven't yet found a need for this particular skill, teach yourself now.

If there is a computer available and a resident parent who will help, Skype (and a growing number of similar services) has a lot more to offer all ages than an ordinary phone. You need to sign up but it doesn't cost anything and calls are free however far apart you are and however long they last. A teenage friend in the South of England did a series of chemistry practice papers on Skype with her dad in Australia. Video-calls are especially valuable to the very young, though, because you and your child can see each other. That's enormously important if you have to be away from a very small child for days or even weeks at a time because it will help her to hang on to a clear image of you. A somewhat older child can show you the gap where her tooth came out or his first barber's haircut. If the cameras are properly adjusted at either end, you can even show picture books and read stories on Skype.

Emails are also invaluable, not only for words but for sharing photos. Whether your child uses a laptop, a smartphone or a tablet, it will probably be worth getting her an email address of her own. If you plan to write to her a lot do make sure that she will check her emails often.

Social networking sites such as Facebook keep millions of people in touch with each other but children cannot use them until they are 13 years old, and even then may not want a parent potentially mixed up with their peers. If your child has a smartphone, he can use its camera to take pictures of things he wants to show you, email them to you and get an immediate voice or voicemail reaction. That isn't social networking but it's certainly contact.

8   When contact fails

Everybody who is professionally involved with separating parents – such as researchers, social workers, solicitors and the family courts – takes the view that it is in children's best interests to have contact with both parents, the non-resident parent as well as the parent they live with, and that it is parents' responsibility to make sure that they do. This book goes somewhat further. What it calls 'separating better' is largely concerned with the relationships parents can make with each other, and the parenting plans they can put in place to ensure not just that the children stay in contact with them both but that they both go on being mother or father to them.

Problems around contact are inevitable, and commonplace ones that contribute to 'separating worse' have been dealt with in earlier chapters. But the ultimate problem, fortunately not at all commonplace, is not just difficulties around contact between child and non-resident parent but absolute refusal of it. That is the subject of this chapter.

8.1   Willing parent & reluctant child

In law, contact with both parents is a child's right and not a parent's. The welfare and best interests of a child are the most important of a court's considerations and the wishes and feelings of children are part of that. However, that doesn't mean that children can choose whether to have contact with a parent or not. How much, if any, notice is taken of children's feelings or choices theoretically depends on their age and level of understanding but in practise also depends on the individual professionals who are involved in a particular case. There is no set age at which a child's wishes will be taken into account by a court but it is unlikely that attention will be paid to the views of very young children as they are thought to be too immature to understand and make decisions about contact. The views of older children – especially teenagers – may be taken more seriously but, in the eyes of some resident parents, are often not taken seriously enough. Courts take the view that unless there is an officially recognised child protection issue, it is the responsibility of parents to encourage their child to take part in contact *whatever the child's feelings about the matter.*

Mother of girl aged 14

" *She dreads seeing him. Really dreads going to that centre place and sitting and talking to him. But still she has to go every three weeks and I have to take her. If I didn't I'd be in breach of a court order. They could even send me to prison I think.* "

No child is old enough to voice a decision about contact if that means choosing which of his parents he prefers to live with or how much time he wants to spend with each. No child should even be asked to make such agonising choices, especially knowing that everything he says will be shared with both parents. But no child who can speak fluently is too young to express his feelings about seeing the non-resident parent and these should certainly be heard – as they are when a full assessment of the family dynamics and patterns of attachment are made – and fed into the court's adult decision-making. Unfortunately such assessments are not always ordered, or carried out, by relevantly trained professionals.

Many parents say that when their child resisted seeing the parent she didn't live with, they found themselves in double trouble. When contact had been ordered by the court, or had been arranged in mediation and would come to court if it didn't work out, they were held responsible for making it happen and if it didn't happen they were held to blame. Convincing a mediator or CAFCASS worker that she had done her best to get the child to contact but the child really refused to go did not get the resident parent off the hook. On the contrary, it was assumed that if the child completely rejected contact with the other parent it could only be because the resident parent had put her off (see Chapter 6.3).

The Family Justice Council has recently recommended that young people should participate more fully in the court process by, for example, writing to the judge or even seeing him. But many professionals in divorce work are against this.

Contact with a non-resident parent works best when child and parent look forward to seeing each other and enjoy being together. If that has never been the case for your family, or if it was the case for a while but the child has now begun to protest about visits and says that he doesn't want to go, don't let the situation drag on. The more time passes since child and parent spent time together, the more reluctant the child will probably become. There are many reasons why children refuse contact and it's important to come to understand, as quickly as possible, what kind of problem is putting your child off. Is it to do with what he feels about the other parent or is it to do with what he feels about you

When did you last see your father?

" [C]hildren often make allegations about their parents which are not credible; children can feel unable to express their view or may even be unable to form their own view of a matter so their expressed wishes and feelings may be misleading.

A child may express the view that s/he does not wish to see their parent; this view may reflect a negative view of the non-resident parent by the parent with day to day care which may be reinforced by that parent's immediate circle of family and friends. Sometimes other professionals are also enlisted by the resident parent who may for example tell a GP or school that the child suffers from stomach cramps, headaches or bedwetting prior to visits with the other parent. "

Ian Kirkland Weir, Hertfordshire Family Forum

Neves Solicitors LLP, 08-07-13

(and leaving you)? Or is the problem something specific about the circumstances of his visits?

- Encourage your child to talk about what he feels about seeing the other parent. Even a four-year-old may be able to explain why he doesn't want to talk to him or visit. Sometimes unwillingness to spend time with the other parent may hinge on specific things that can be changed and put right, such as always having to share the visit with the parent's future partner.
- Try not to let the child pick up on your own thoughts or feelings about the man who is your ex-partner but his current-and-forever dad. As we have seen, you don't have to intend to alienate a child to do so (see Chapter 6.2). Children often refuse contact as a result of subtle messages about the parent they are supposed to visit that they have picked up from the parent they live with. If you are furiously angry and upset with your ex it is really difficult for a child who lives with you and loves you to put your feelings aside and look forward to seeing and loving him. You may be able to make it possible for the child to love you both if you spell out to him, in whatever way he is old enough to understand, the difference between his father's partnership with you (which has failed and made you furious) and his parenting of the child which hasn't failed and makes you happy (see Chapter 5).
- Force yourself to face the fact that whether he shows it in conventional ways or not your child is experiencing real grief at the loss not only of the parent who doesn't live with him anymore but also of the two of you together: his parents as he knew them. However hard you try, neither of you is the same parent (or the same person) as you were before the family broke up, and your child's rejection of the contact arranged for him may be part of a refusal to accept what feels to him so much a second best.
- Understand that an agony of conflict and split loyalty is inevitable for your child. He loves you both yet every sign of love for one feels like disloyalty to the other. He may be unable to feel comfortable with the other parent because visits inevitably involve hugs, and hugs make him feel guilty.
- Recognise that your child's reactions to contact with his other parent are almost certainly linked to the relationship between the two of you now, and will continue to be so. The better the relationship and the more mutual your parenting (see Chapter 5.1) the less likely it is that a child will refuse contact. Conversely, the fact that your child is refusing contact suggests that the two of you are not on good terms or perhaps are not on terms at all. Do try to keep (or reinstate) some kind of communication with your ex so that the two of you can discuss what the real problem is and what is to be done.

Reasons for children refusing contact

Handovers

If your child makes clear his refusal to take part in a visit with the non-resident parent, even while it is only in prospect and hasn't yet begun, it may be that the very beginning is most of the problem. Maybe the child would be perfectly happy with his father once the two of them were together and without you. But you can only find that out if you can deal with the handover.

Whether children are collected from home or from a neutral place, or driven to the father's home or chosen meeting place, handover times are often the most difficult parts of contact visits for younger children. Even older children (who are expected to go rather than be handed over) sometimes find the actual transition from one parent to the other very conflicting, so some degree of difficulty is commonplace. As we have seen (see Chapter 6.2) there are many ways you can help, from making the handover quick and smooth with no lingering goodbyes, to dropping off or collecting a child from a neutral place, such as school or a relative's house. Wherever you are trying to hand him over a young child may adamantly refuse to leave you, clinging to your leg or your skirt and keeping his head buried so as not to see his father. If he is small enough he could be (and some children are) literally 'handed over', screaming and struggling. Although that may be a quick solution for today, and if he is calm and happy the moment they are out of your sight, it may seem like the right thing to do, but it is not a good way to make a child feel that leaving mum is safe and going with dad is fun. In fact a child who is physically forced is likely to remember his fear and frustration and anticipate those horrible feelings next time a visit is proposed. An older child may meet insistence that he go on a contact visit with passive resistance. A teenager will often refuse contact by locking himself in his room and refusing to appear for the intended handover or journey. Occasionally an older child or teenager who is ambivalent about both parents and the contact they have arranged for him will turn the tables on them by going with his father, as planned, and then refusing to return home at the end of a visit.

Problems at handover obviously affect (and are enormously distressing for) you both. Don't try to sort them out in front of the child. If this is the first time it's come up and you haven't planned how to cope it may be best not to go on trying to force the issue this time but arrange to talk to your ex about it later. If you are not on direct telephoning terms you'll need to enlist whoever has helped you in mediation or specifically in making access arrangements. It is urgent. If you allow visits to go on starting with hysterical distress, or if you allow the distress to cancel the visits, the relationship between father and child (and between you and the father) can only get worse.

Secret fears

Sometimes a child has a reason for refusing contact which she is unwilling or unable to tell you about. Reasons sometimes include previous physical, sexual or emotional abuse or the child having felt frighteningly unsafe during earlier contact.

Adult woman looking back to when she was 11

> " *My little sister and I had to spend three weeks of the summer holidays with our father. He never actually did anything wrong but I was always terrified that he would. Like if I forgot something (there was a gate I always forgot to shut) he'd say 'what shall I do? Shall I spank you?' Or when I came out of the bath (the bathroom was downstairs) in pyjamas he'd say 'There's my pretty girl; come and give a lonely man a big cuddle.' I know it sounds harmless but it wasn't. But how could I have explained to my mum?* "

No child should be compelled into contact that frightens her or makes her anxious and uneasy. If this seems to be the case an expert assessment of each family member in relation to the others needs to be carried out so as to establish not only the facts but also the feelings of all concerned. Does the other parent press for regular visits with the child because he loves and misses her or is his motive concerned with keeping control over you? Does the child really hate his father as he says, or does he think you will be pleased if he says that? Talk to a solicitor or to CAFCASS about assessment and the possibility of a subsequent application to the court for an order restricting contact.

Separation anxiety

The most common reason for serious problems over contact is separation anxiety, which is global rather than specific and is not due to any inappropriate behaviour by the parent. Most babies and toddlers are liable to get anxious when they are parted from the parent they are most attached to. Contact with the non-resident parent (usually dad) almost always means leaving mum and home. Crying, clinging and tantrums are normal reactions to separation, from late in the first year until around four years old, but the intensity and timing vary widely from child to child. Some children will go on getting anxious about leaving you (or having you leave them) all through the primary school years. That's what those Sunday night blues or Monday morning tummy-aches are about.

In intact families and ordinary circumstances separation anxiety becomes less frequent and less intense as the child grows up. In the meantime you can do a lot to ease it by combining being understanding and sympathetic with your child's anxious feelings with being firm and clear that what is being asked of him is safe and what he should do.

Mother of boy aged 6

For a while he got so upset about school and I got so upset at having to leave him crying in his classroom that I wondered if I should let him have a break at home with me. But children do have to go to school don't they? It seemed better that he should face that… By half-term he only cried on Monday mornings and by the next term he didn't cry at all!

Some children's separation anxiety doesn't just go away and stay away, though, but lasts for months or years and is so severe that it gets in the way of all the child's normal activities, developing into what many health professionals call 'separation anxiety disorder'. Developmentally normal separation anxiety shares many signs and symptoms with separation anxiety disorder, but they differ in the intensity of your child's fears and how little it takes to set them off. If your child is moving into separation anxiety disorder, being left alone in bed while you go downstairs may cause panic, and just the thought of leaving the house without you may be enough to upset her.

Separation anxiety is about a child feeling unsafe. In the very early years your child's attachment to you means that she feels unsafe whenever you aren't there or available to her if she needs you (see Chapter 2). Later on, and if the more extreme separation anxiety disorder develops, it will be because something has thrown the child off-balance; made her feel threatened and unable to cope or to manage herself and her world and therefore to feel extra-dependent on you to do it for her.

Many different life-events can play a part in increasing normal separation anxiety or tipping a susceptible child towards separation anxiety disorder. But other than the death of a parent, nothing is more likely to bring those separate events together than parental separation.

When you separate your child may face:

- loss of a parent
- loss of other love-objects such as caregivers or pets
- changes in her environment such as a new house, school or day-care nursery

- the stress associated with all the above changes
- your anxiety and distress which she will sense and which will feed her own.

If your child's separation anxiety is within ordinary limits except that it is inappropriate to their age, there is a lot you can do to help him to feel safer, especially if the other parent will play their part.

- Practice separation. Make contact visits very brief at first, then gradually extend them as the child becomes more positive (or less anxious) about leaving you to go with dad.
- For babies and toddlers, schedule contact visits for times of day when the child is at his most calm and cheerful – often in the second half of the afternoon after lunch and a nap.
- Have a special 'goodbye' ritual that you use whenever the child is separated from you and which he will therefore find reassuring when he leaves you to go with the other parent. Don't spin the leave-taking out though. Keep it as brief as a hug, a kiss on the nose and a few words such as 'Love you. See you soon. Have fun.'
- Try to have the separation take place in familiar surroundings. If contact cannot start from home without raising your stress-level intolerably, try making the handover in another neutral, familiar place such as a grandparent's home.
- When a small child leaves, make sure he takes a familiar and beloved toy or cuddly with him (but make sure the other parent realises it is important and doesn't let it get lost during the outing).
- However upset the child is, try not to give in and let him stay at home with you after all. He needs to know that you and the other parent are both confident that he will be OK and have a good time without you.

Separation anxiety disorder

The above tips may do something to help the child with separation anxiety disorder and will certainly do no harm. But it is important to realise how much more serious separation anxiety disorder is than separation anxiety.

Your child will feel constantly worried – every hour of every day – in case something happens that leads to him being separated from you and acutely fearful when something does. The fear that overwhelms him will probably be one or more of the following:

- Fear that if he goes away something terrible will happen to someone he loves; most commonly that terrible harm (an accident, an illness, a murder, insanity) will come to you while

Grandmother recalls herself aged 7

Every day, coming home on the bus, I'd see myself going in by the kitchen door and mummy being there but quite mad so she didn't recognise me.

he is gone. When children cannot leave home to go to school, it is not entirely school they fear but what may happen to a parent in their absence.

- Worry that once he is separated from you, something – such as getting lost or being kidnapped – will happen to make the separation permanent.
- Nightmares about being taken away from you or about losing you in a forest or watching you vanish into the sea.

Because of these fears a child with separation anxiety disorder may:

- Refuse to go anywhere without you. That means that he not only refuses planned contact with the other parent but also school and play dates with friends.
- Be extremely reluctant to be left alone in bed and terrified to go to sleep.
- Suffer from a range of psychosomatic complaints such as headaches and tummy-aches.
- Prefer to be within touch or sight of you all the time so that if he is small he may literally cling on to you as you move around and if he is older he may shadow you from room to room, even waiting for you outside the bathroom like a toddler.

What you can do to help the child with separation anxiety disorder

Anything you can do to make your child feel safer in herself, her life, her home and her relationships can help. Even if you cannot completely solve the problem, your understanding and sympathy can only make things better.

- Find out all you can about separation anxiety disorder and what your child is suffering so that it is clear to her that you understand. Older children in particular recognise that their fears are fantastical and are afraid of not being taken seriously.
- Listen carefully to anything your child will tell you about her feelings. Encourage her to talk; there's nothing to be gained by trying not to think about it.
- Remind the child – gently – that despite all that angst, he or she survived the last separation and all the separations before it.
- Anticipate times that are likely to cause separation difficulty and try different ways of helping. If your child finds it easier to separate from you at home than at the school gate, get a friend to take her to school instead of you and get your ex to start contact visits from the friend's home.

Girl aged 10

" *You know what makes a really big, huge difference? Knowing that mum will be there to meet me when school or something else I have to do without her finishes. Just thinking about her waiting at the gate really helps. I know it's babyish being met but she says 'better met than absent'!* "

- Provide as consistent a daily pattern at home as you can. Don't underestimate the importance of predictability for children with separation anxiety problems. If the contact arrangements are going to change or a visitor is coming to stay, discuss it with your child ahead of time. During the months when anxiety is acute, try not to accept work or social commitments at such short notice that the child unexpectedly finds that you are not at home.
- Be careful not to let your child's anxiety buy endless indulgence. She needs your sympathy but she needs behavioural boundaries too or her life is likely to become more and more restricted. Let your child know that although you understand her feelings about going to bed, to school or on contact visits, she does have to go, and remind her how well she managed last time.
- Offering the child choices or elements of control in an activity or interaction with an adult may help him or her to feel safer and more comfortable. She has to go to her Saturday music class: how would she prefer to manage the journey and being there without you?

Your own patience and know-how can certainly help your child with separation anxiety disorder, but it may not be enough, especially in a family breakdown situation. Some children with separation anxiety disorder need professional intervention. Assessments carried out by CAFCASS for the court or by Expert Witnesses will establish whether your child is one of these.

8.2 Willing child & reluctant parent

Almost all the parents who abandon contact with their children are fathers. Not only are there many fewer non-resident mothers, but research statistics from many countries show that they are very much more likely to stay in touch with their children year after year and through thick and thin.

If a non-resident father doesn't want to see his child, or even have indirect contact with her, there is nothing the mother can do to make him. He is legally obliged to pay 'child support' but that's only money, it's nothing to do with emotional support or contact. It seems ironic that a mother is legally obliged to encourage even the most reluctant children to have contact with their willing fathers, but has no legal support for keeping willing children in touch with non-resident fathers who don't want them.

Many of the men who have no contact with their children had no more than passing contact with the mothers. If the two parents never lived together and the father only saw the baby a few times (or not at all), his vanishing act will not affect the child as badly as being deserted by a father who is known and loved. Don't assume, though, that a child you have brought up on your own will not want to know who his father is and why he didn't stick around. Some mothers who marry within a year or two of a child's birth wonder if it is necessary for him to know that his stepfather (who may become his adoptive father) is not his biological father. All the evidence is that a child should know the truth as soon as you judge him old enough. It is not only necessary because we all need to know our backgrounds and where we came from, but also because lies within families almost always come out. If your child eventually discovers (perhaps because you and his stepfather eventually separate) that the man he has always called daddy is not his natural father, he will feel that the whole of his childhood has been thrown into uncertainty and everything he knew or felt about his family was false.

The next largest group of vanishing fathers consists of the many whose parenting after separation is not mutual or polite but broken and eventually non-existent. These are often men who get so worn down by the difficulties of negotiating with their exes and keeping to contact schedules with their children that they give up. Often regular weekends gradually become irregular invitations, and daytime or holiday visits become unpredictable and rare. Eventually they just don't happen anymore. For a while – and especially if mothers keep pressing for contact – the easier kinds, such as phone calls and texts, may carry on for a while. But a vicious circle operates such that as contact dwindles it becomes more of an effort. What do you say in a quick text to a 14-year-old you haven't spoken to in six months?

Boy now aged 16

> I haven't seen my dad since I was 13. For the longest time – like years – I went on being thrilled when he turned up and believing his excuses when he didn't. My mum was really good about that. But then there was a birthday when he didn't even send a card, and then another birthday, and then I sort of realised he'd gone. I wish I knew where he's gone because I really need to ask him what I did to make him just not care about me.

The last group of vanishing fathers – and thankfully the smallest – are men who just decide to go. Some of them leave the country and make a new kid-free start. Some of them have girlfriends who wouldn't want anything to do with a child from an earlier relationship. Some of them hope that if they stop seeing the children they can stop paying. Not all these vanishing fathers jump out of their children's lives entirely of their own accord, though. Some of them are worn down by ceaseless criticism and disapproval, low-level alienation perhaps, from their exes. A few are pushed out by the children's mothers and either do not realise that they can seek help with access from the court, or cannot face – or afford – a continuing struggle (see Chapter 6).

However it comes about, the loss to children whose parents vanish is almost worse than actual bereavement. If a father dies it's not because he wanted to leave and even children, guilt-prone though they are, cannot believe that it's their fault he had a heart attack or crashed his car. But if a father just leaves it is obviously because he chooses to and the fact that he made that choice tells his child that she is somehow to blame: she wasn't clever enough or good enough; she wasn't loveable enough or she didn't tell her father she loved him often enough. Grief and guilt is a toxic combination and most mothers really struggle to find an alternative set of explanations that make sense but are less painful for the heartbroken child. When she says 'why doesn't daddy come and see me or ring me up any more?' There isn't an answer that won't hurt. If it's clear that your ex really has dumped the child you probably can't do better than explain that when things have gone very wrong for people they sometimes feel that they have to get themselves out of it however they can and without thinking about how much other people will be hurt. You might want to say that behaving that way isn't admirable but certainly doesn't suggest that the child has done anything wrong. If you think your child is old enough to want to understand a little more you might want to add that the only two people who were responsible for things going wrong and breaking-up the family were her father and yourself and that you apologise for both of you for not having managed to stay together or to separate better.

Being in contact with both parents gives children a sense of their own identity. When one parent doesn't wish to be involved in the child's life, knowing *about* him is better than nothing. Try to make it clear to the child that you are able to talk about his father without getting too distressed, and make sure that your child has photos of himself with his father. If you can manage to remain on friendly terms with your absent ex's extended family, contact with his paternal grandparents may help too.

One day your child may decide to try and trace their other parent, just as many adopted children do. Just as it's tough for adoptive parents to see a child going all out to find someone who's had no contact with her for 18 years during which they have been loving and caring for her, so watching your beloved child trying to trace a vanished dad who walked out on her leaving you to be mother and father in one can leave you seething with sorrow and resentment. Try to work through all those bad feelings and come up feeling good about yourself, though, because if your child finds her dad she may get rejected all over again and then she will desperately need your support.

Part III

What Works & What Does Not

9 More issues parents raise

Parents who separate often have to face practical and emotional problems that none of their advisers had mentioned and make decisions that they therefore hadn't thought about in advance. Some of them have shared the issues that were most important to their children and the solutions they eventually arrived at.

9.1 High days & holidays

The routines and rhythms of life as a family with children are punctuated by special occasions. All families quickly accumulate their own ceremonies and ways of celebrating them, which children expect and look forward to. It's not only the big personally important days like birthdays, or public holidays that are celebrated almost everywhere such as Christmas, New Year and Easter, or holidays that come from particular countries, such as Thanksgiving from the USA or St Patrick's day from Ireland, that are important. There are also religious holidays such as Eid and Yom Kippur that matter very much to particular groups of families and a few which are part of the very fabric of daily life for some, such as Shabbat to observant Jews. And as well as all of those there are many lower-key 'special days' which your family may or may not have chosen to celebrate such as Valentine's Day, Mother's Day or Halloween.

Just as important as many of those – if not more so – are occasions that individual families invent and celebrate for themselves, like a special dinner to mark the last night of each school term. Any of these – and many others – may have become part of the fabric of your children's family lives, and if family life has disintegrated what is to become of them? Birthdays still happen of course but they may not feel celebratory with one parent (and a sad one at that) taking part instead of two. Christmas dominates schools and high streets but the inescapable carols make separated adults and older children think nostalgically about last year and younger children sober at their sad faces. And what about the family's own fun breaks: will Sunday lunch with grandparents and Friday movie-nights carry on now that the routines of daily life that they used to break up are no longer in place? Everybody loses so much when a family breaks down that losing high days and holidays may sound trivial. It doesn't feel trivial to children, though. Losing those eagerly anticipated punctuation marks in ordinary life that they used to plan for will leave holes in children's lives, and the desperate difficulty of finding ways to replace or keep on with them is something that many parents struggle with.

The best way to rescue the special days that matter most to your family from the doldrums of divorce is to be proactive in changing exactly how you celebrate them. The actions that are open to you crucially depend on circumstances, of course, and on how much energy and headspace you can muster. If you separated in April and it's now October you may not be able to bear even to think about Christmas. But even if you don't think about it, Christmas will come and cannot be ignored. You all have to get through it somehow and how you do that will really matter to any child who is old enough to remember last year.

The circumstance that matters most is your relationship with each other as parents. Specifically, whether you can ever be in the same place at the same time so that the children can have you both on occasions that are really important to them. If sharing space is a step too far, can your children at least have the benefit of your shared thinking about them – including what one wants for his birthday or what another plans to put on a list to Father Christmas? Even if the answer to both questions is a less polite version of 'no!' you can still be proactive, but it will be a great deal easier if the answer is 'yes'. The following ways forward come highly recommended:

- Instead of trying to make the big holidays such as Christmas or Thanksgiving just as they have always been but with only one parent, turn outwards and put the emphasis on making it an extended family day; his family as well as yours, if any relations live near enough. If there are any who live within reach but have not been on speaking terms with you since the separation, this is the kind of initiative that often breaks down those barriers. Even if people are scattered this idea can work if there is somebody in the family with the will to adopt it. There may be one person with a large home who can and will host a family get-together, or someone who will rent a winter short-break cottage for you all. Once you float the idea you may be surprised by how many people there are who would welcome it and be prepared to travel for it, not just for yours and the children's sakes but for their own as well.

Paternal grandmother of boy aged 2, and two girls aged 4 and 6

We'll not go, that's for sure. Well we won't, will we? I mean I wouldn't go to her home after the way she's treated our Jake… but I do miss those little monsters and if he'll be there – well maybe we could…

- Making the 'family' in family celebration into 'extended family' means, of course, that the other parent is welcome to come and take part and the fact that people from his side of the family are invited should make it easier for him to accept. Even if he refuses to take part in the planning he'll be kept fully informed of the plans, and if in the end he doesn't come his absence will be far less noticeable in a crowd gathered in a different place than it would have been at home. It is not that his children won't miss their daddy, of course; he's irreplaceable. But because their Christmas or Thanksgiving doesn't rely on you and him but on you and other family members, his absence is less likely to mean that it all falls apart.
- Opening up the tight little world of the nuclear family can work even if you have no actual extended family to open up to. Among your close friends with children in the same age groups as yours it's very likely that there are one or two who are in a similar situation and would welcome pooling support and resources for some occasions. And if you know someone who is completely on their own, an invitation to Christmas dinner at your home might transform the holiday not only for them but also for you and the children, because entertaining guests makes everything different.

Mother of girl aged 8 and boy aged 6

" " *Last Christmas was just after we split up and we spent it here, sort of trying to copy the year before. It was horrible. One of the worst days of the whole separation. This year had to be different. We don't have family in this country and although friends invited us my daughter wanted to be at home for Christmas day so we thought instead of having an empty place at table we'll fill it up. We invited an elderly neighbour who has a little dog the children simply loved and a young woman who's on her own with a baby (the children liked the baby too but not as much as the dog). She's now my precious babysitter. It wasn't just a really good day, it was also a day that made me realise I could still do nice and worthwhile things with and for the children on my own.* " "

If one of these ideas works for you one year it could be the pattern for years to come, cementing relationships with your children's wider family or your community; enlarging your

Younger married sister

" " *Our Lily's only nine months so Christmas at home seems a bit silly. She isn't going to open a stocking or eat turkey. So we'd probably have gone to mum and dad's but this way we can all be together and it'll be great.* " "

Paternal great aunt

" " *Our son is grown and he and his family are in New Zealand. It's years since we had a proper houseful and children at Christmas.* " "

friendship group and ensuring that your children never have to eat two Christmas or Thanksgiving dinners.

- Birthdays really matter to children and many report being hurt or offended by birthday arrangements that were made over their heads to suit separated parents. The problem is that children's birthdays are important to parents too, so there is often competition between mother and father over who a child will be with for the big day. Sometimes parents insist that the two of them should have the birthday child on alternate years. Sometimes the arrangement is that she will celebrate her birthday in whichever household she happens to be.

If the two of you are ever going to get together to make an occasion for your children, birthdays are excellent occasions to make the effort. Some separated parents whose children are school age or older swear by a birthday dinner in a restaurant for the child and his best friend(s) because as well as being a big treat for the birthday child, being in public and in a formal setting helps parents to be polite.

There are other ways for your child to have both of you involved in a birthday that don't mean you have to set eyes on each other. In intact families, when a child's actual birthday falls on a school day it is often split from birthday celebrations which need to take place at the weekend. That same idea can work for separated parents, with the parent the child mostly lives with doing the actual birthday and the other parent laying on a birthday trip or treat for the next visit. A birthday party will need to be held close to home, school and guests and either at a weekend or in the holidays, so if a child normally goes to her father every weekend and the birthday falls in term time, this is one of the occasions when regular contact arrangements need you to be friendly and flexible (see Chapter 5.1).

- A lot of celebrations such as Guy Fawkes or Halloween are actually more fun for children when more people are involved, and you don't always have to be the one who lays things on. There may be a get-together that a school gate or nursery friend or acquaintance is helping with hosting and to which you and yours would be welcome. Or there may be a community gathering which, especially for November 5th, offers more and safer bangs for each buck. The idea is that doing *something* special keeps the occasion fun for your children, but that not doing the same as you used to do makes it easier for you.
- You don't have to keep up every single one of your previous family's private celebratory traditions. There are probably

Young man aged 20

" *The birthday thing made me furious all through my teens. How dare they say I'd got to stay with mum for it this year 'because it's her turn'? My birthday, not anybody else's turn.* "

some that your children will not notice or miss. But some – maybe the chocolate egg trail through the nearest piece of open country at Easter, or the barbecue that celebrates the last night of the school year – do also lend themselves to being shared with other families. Children often know surprisingly little about each other's home circumstances but there's a good chance that some of your children's friends have parents in a similar position to theirs. Discovering that, and spending time together as two still-surviving families, may be helpful to all the children and to you adults as well.

Summer holidays

Parenting agreements, whether made by the court, worked out with mediators or agreed privately by parents, often include the right for the non-resident parent to take the children on a summer holiday. All the considerations that apply to overnight or weekend contact with the other parent also apply to going on holiday (see Chapter 7.3).

Holidays do provoke particular difficulties though. A lot might have arisen if your family had remained intact – these are family holiday problems rather than post-separation problems – but if one of you is going to cope with them alone it's as well to be aware of them.

- A teenage girl may much prefer the company of peers to parents and may not want to come. If she is made to come she may sulk, brilliantly.
- A teenage boy may not be so devoted to his peers but will only look forward to a holiday that has planned goals, and will very likely enjoy one only if it has physical activities.
- Primary school-aged children are probably the easiest to please and the same kinds of holiday will often suit both girls and boys, but a single child is likely to be lonely and bored and extremely hard work for the parent who must also be playmate. If it's financially possible to work it out, inviting a school friend along can work well.
- Most children are reluctant sightseers (so might not think there is much to do in cities) and many get very bored on long car journeys. Children under about eight seem almost incapable of being interested in anything they see out of the windows of a moving car so if you want them to get anything out of going through those mountains or seeing those wild horses, you have to allow the time to keep stopping so they can get out.

Problems that are specific to non-resident fathers taking children on holiday are most likely to arise when you are taking a very young child, or when you are taking several children of different genders and very mixed ages.

- Whatever his age, if a child already looks forward to, and enjoys, staying overnight with you, there is every reason to suppose that you can successfully holiday together. But if a child is under four – especially if he is a baby or toddler – and not yet accustomed to staying with you away from mother and home, a holiday may not be the best way for either of you to start. Not only will the child be away from his mum, he will also be staying in novel surroundings – whether hotel, B&B, rented apartment, caravan or tent – which he may find strange and bewildering, eating different food and living without his accustomed routine. You will therefore be caring for him on your own for the first time in circumstances where he will probably be unusually needy or demanding. Start with a brief trial run such as a holiday weekend, and try for a home-like environment such as a farm guesthouse.
- If a child is approaching seven and seems ready to spend a real holiday with you, keep the first one fairly brief – a week away from mother and home is enough – and stay within easy travelling distance. Roughly 10% of this age group are liable to become overwhelmingly homesick and if yours should be one of them, you need to be able to bring her home. Several fathers who have been through this warn that if you are on a package holiday in another country, flight restrictions may mean that you cannot cut the trip short. If a child is forced to go on with the holiday when she is desperate to go home she won't remember the bits she enjoyed such as the lovely beaches, the warm sea and the best-ever ice cream. Her recollection of the whole holiday will be dominated by memories of her misery and the next time you suggest a holiday she probably will not want to come.
- If she is accustomed to coming to stay with you at the same time as older siblings, make sure that at least one of them is included in the holiday.
- Agree with your ex that the child will be allowed – and helped – to contact her while she is away if she wants to. A brief daily goodnight phone or Skype call may really help her; on the other hand it may actually provoke homesickness. Make sure that any calls she makes are for her benefit rather than for her mother's.
- If there is only one child involved in a holiday and she or he is older – ten or over perhaps – it should be possible to think of a trip that is tailored to him or her and affordable and at least tolerable to you. Your 14-year-old daughter may always have longed to go to Paris by Eurostar, for example, while a

Girl aged 7

"When I'd had too much sun and I felt sick I told dad I wanted my mum and I wanted to go home. He was OK with it and went to ask about flights but when he came back and said we absolutely couldn't go till the end of the week I got really upset. I think it was knowing we couldn't that was the bad part."

13-year-old son wants to cycle or climb and a nine-year-old only wants to be by the sea. You may be willing, even eager, to do any of those things but you can only do them one at a time, so if you are taking several children on holiday you will have to find a compromise destination that offers at least something each child will enjoy. If you were one of two adults, you could then share yourselves out, taking turns so that each child could do the things they liked most. But as a single parent on holiday with two or three children you are up against a real difficulty, which is that because you are on your own everybody has to do the same things at the same time, whether they like it or not. And sometimes they won't.

- Some separated fathers turn to their own parents, either to join in holidays with the children or, if they have plenty of space and enough for children to do, to provide them. If money is not a problem, sharing rented holiday accommodation with grandparents can work well for everybody, giving all three generations a chance to live together for a few days.

- Some parents recommend packages that offer exciting children's clubs and so many supervised activities – from water sports to disco dancing – that any older child will find something to enjoy at any moment of the day. Holiday villages (there are hundreds of them advertising on the internet) pride themselves on this. However, shy children may find it difficult to join in. And these holidays are far from cheap.

- If you are going it alone, beaches and sea are probably your best bet provided you go somewhere the sun is likely to shine, so that if your teenage daughter is not in the mood for bathing in cold water (even in a wetsuit) she can sunbathe instead. Do allow for the fact that children under about 12 cannot safely be allowed in the sea for a single minute without an adult, even if they are strong swimmers (probably in a swimming pool), nor be trusted to stay out of the sea until you get back from taking their smaller sibling to the toilet. Meeting the demands of everyone's safety and enjoyment make a beach a highly stressful place for a single parent. If a small child wants to make sandcastles and a bigger one wants to swim, one adult isn't enough unless you also have a teenager who will help supervise younger ones.

- Most people agree that it's easier for two adults to supervise six children (and stay sane) than for one adult to supervise two or three, so you might consider sharing the holiday with another similarly-placed family.

9.2 Pressures toward independence from adults

As if coping with no longer being a spouse was not difficult enough, the practicalities of daily life as a suddenly single parent can take you unawares and need a lot of organising. Even if the children's care has always fallen mostly to you, their father probably played a far bigger part than was obvious until he was gone. Because he was in the house you could leave one child while you fetched or did something with another when need arose; leave them all playing while you made an efficiency trip to the supermarket or get him to pick up the teenager from her party while you did the baby's late-evening feed. Now that there isn't a second adult in the house you will often need to be in two places at once.

Why is this any different for separated families than for families that have been single-parent for years – or perhaps from the beginning? Parents say that it's different because single parenting after separation is a new situation and change of lifestyle that contradicts the experience and expectations of both resident adult and children. It raises many questions they haven't needed to address before and many of them are to do with whether or not children are old enough to be unsupervised.

Parents' views of appropriate ages for children to be unsupervised

Average ages given by parents for:

Walking to school alone: ten years (National Walk to School Campaign gives no specific age – only parents' judgement of child and route)

Staying home alone for 'a few hours': 13 years (though some said 8; some said 18)

Minimum age to take a train alone: 13 years

Youngest age for an unaccompanied plane journey: 14 years

Youngest age to be left alone at home overnight: 15 years

Youngest age at which it is appropriate for a child to be left at home for a weekend: 17 years

Thompson, 2011

Being at home alone

When mothers and fathers both have jobs outside their homes they often fill any gaps between their working hours and children's school hours between them. The most usual gap is between the end of the school day and the end of the work-and-travel day, but gaps between leaving times in the morning are also commonplace, often with mother leaving early (so as to get home early) and father seeing children off to school before leaving himself. Father moving out, or mother and children living somewhere else without him, means that there's only half the adult gap-filling power.

All these gaps raise the same question: is this particular child old enough to cope on his own? Will he be all right letting himself into an empty house and being there alone for a couple of hours? Or, will she cope with being left on her own at breakfast time and getting herself off to school (locking the front door behind her)?

- There's no legal ruling on the age your child must reach before he can be left alone. The NSPCC (National Society for the Prevention of Cruelty to Children) suggests that 13 is the youngest age at which a child is likely to be mature enough to cope with an emergency and therefore no child younger than that should be left 'for more than a very short time'. They don't spell out the 'very short time' but it's clear they are measuring in minutes rather than in hours. Whatever a child's age (if he is under 16) you can be prosecuted for wilful neglect if you leave him 'in a manner likely to cause unnecessary suffering or injury to health'; otherwise it is up to you – and the other parent.
- A great many under-13s from 'intact families' as well as single-parent homes do come back from school to empty houses and occupy themselves until a parent comes home. However, it may be somewhat more of a challenge for your 11- or 12-year old, not only because he isn't used to it but also because it emphasises the loneliness that he is probably already feeling because of the other parent's absence. In fact, an important consideration in this and all other 'home alone' situations is what the child feels about it. A big study of 'latch-key children' in the United States found that a sadly high percentage of them dreaded the time spent alone in the house and many were anxious, even frightened, especially in winter when they returned to a house in darkness.
- It's very unlikely that a child who is not yet old enough for secondary school will cope safely and comfortably with coming home to an empty house. If you are seriously considering this for an eight- or nine-year-old ask yourself

Father of boy aged 9 and girl aged 11

" *I don't know how she'll manage. I drive a cab and I've always been able to take a break to meet the kids from school or pick my daughter up from school clubs and stuff. My wife – I should say my ex-wife – doesn't get home until six so I don't know what she'll do.* "

whether you are sure he can remember to take the door key with him, remember where he has put it and, above all, easily persuade it to turn. Once in the house, does he know where all the light switches are? Can he get himself a snack? And, above all, can he use the phone? He needs to be able to call you to report that he's safely home and to hear your voice; he needs to be able to phone a friendly adult who is close by (and always in) if he is worried about anything; and he also needs to know that he should dial 999 in any emergency, and that when the person who answers asks him 'what service do you require' she means 'what's up?' and he should tell her. The harsh truth, though, is that if there really is an emergency – the boiler catches fire, the gale blows a window in or there's a burglar upstairs – he will be far too frightened to do anything sensible. If your number is on speed dial he might call you, but you are really gambling on nothing untoward happening; a reasonable bet, perhaps, if he will be alone for 20 minutes; not so good if it will be two hours.

- Two children together are less likely to be lonely and scared but perhaps more likely to get themselves into trouble, either because they quarrel or because a fun game goes pear-shaped.

A ten- and a 13-year-old may be all right on their own for an hour or so but even the 13-year-old should not be expected to look after a much younger sibling (see babysitting, below).

Some parents find better solutions to the gap between hours of adult work and children's school:

- There may be after-school provision designed for exactly this, or there may be after-school activities that fill the gap while fulfilling a different purpose such as drama or gymnastics or football (be wary of the latter – in many schools they rely on the enthusiastic presence of one teacher and are therefore liable to sudden cancellation if she is away). If you have children at more than one school matching up their after-school programmes may be a nightmare.
- If you have good links in the community you may be able to find a much older 'child' – a 17-year-old, perhaps – who has exams coming up and a load of homework but is also keen to earn money and would therefore be pleased to walk your children home and stay with them until you get there.
- In some towns there may be a registered childminder who has opted to concentrate on before- and after-school care and has space to include your children. Some secondary school children feel demeaned by this suggestion but many find a new friendship group in the childminder's home and some go

One of a pair of twin boys then aged 9

> *The worst was the time I locked Joe in the toilet and then couldn't make the key work. He got panicky so I got the stepladder out of the shed so he could climb out of the window. Only the window wasn't big enough and he got stuck. Would I have thought to ring the fire brigade or even the neighbour whose number was written by the phone? Nope. It was pure luck that she heard Joe yelling.*

on dropping in for an after-school snack long after they really *are* old enough to be at home alone.

- If you are very fortunate there may be a grandparent or other relative or relative-in-law who lives locally, does not work full-time and would like to help.
- The very best solution comes with so many 'ifs' that it's rare but: if the children's father lives nearby, his work is flexible or freelance and you and he are trying to be mutual parents, filling those gaps may be his major contribution to everyone's wellbeing.

The home-alone problem is not only about school, of course, but unless their father was the children's full-time carer in the school holidays and not able or prepared to continue to be, your separation will not mean that you have to make new plans. You will be able to go on with whatever arrangements you used to make before the family break-up, and the continuity will be especially welcome to your children.

Young babysitters

The law says nothing about how old a person has to be before he or she can babysit, although the NSPCC recommends a minimum age of 16. If you leave your child with anyone who is younger than 16, you, not the babysitter, remain legally responsible for the child's safety. So while under-16s can babysit, they cannot take legal responsibility for a child and if something dangerous happens to him you will be blamed (and no doubt blame yourself). So, as with leaving children at home alone, leaving them with an under-age babysitter, even their own sibling, is a calculated risk. If there was a fire or a dangerous accident, a child was taken seriously ill or an intruder broke in, there's only another child to cope.

- Know the babysitter. If it's not your own older child but somebody else's, don't employ him or her until he or she is at least 16 and even then try to get some word of mouth recommendations.
- If the prospective babysitter is your own older child, will he take the responsibility seriously? Will the younger child or children do as he says? Does he know how to keep safe at home and who to telephone if he needs help?
- Don't take even this small risk with a baby. Even if she is asleep in her cot she could throw up and choke, or spike a really high fever. She almost certainly won't, but she *could*, and if she did, a very young and inexperienced babysitter wouldn't know what to do.

Mother of two boys aged 18 months and 12 years, and a girl aged 8

❝ *On my own with the baby 24/7 and the other two when they weren't at school I just felt trapped. I couldn't move. Couldn't slip to the shop or have a coffee with my friend next door like I used to while my ex watched the football. So I did get the boy to babysit until their father found out and said he'd tell the social. So now I'm stuck.* ❞

- Don't take the risk with a toddler either; in inexperienced hands he could (and very likely would) put something small enough to choke on in his mouth, which the child in charge probably won't anticipate, or fall over something or down the stairs or off the chair he climbed on. He may or may not bang his head hard enough to matter but it takes experience to judge.
- If you leave a primary school-aged child with a very young babysitter keep the time you're away really short. Children in that age group can have all manner of accidents in the home, of course, but the chances of your child doing so in any single hour are low. You can probably skedaddle to the local shop but not out for the evening.

Many suddenly single mothers count on getting breaks when children go to stay with their father, at weekends or in the holidays. If you have a baby or toddler, or a four- or five-year-old who cannot yet go away happily overnight, try not to let your need for freedom override her need to stay securely with you. Some mothers in this situation have managed to set-up a single-parent babysitting swap scheme. The usual scheme by which couples take it in turns to go out while one parent of another pair babysits their children can only work for couples, but single mothers can take it in turns to go out while another mother and her children babysit for her. Whether they sleep the night or are woken to go home when the mother comes in, both the host children and the babysitting children often much enjoy these necessarily sociable evenings. Other mothers, especially those whose very young children don't settle well in a strange house even if mum is there, resign themselves to going out only when a grandparent can babysit for them. In the meantime they break-up the feeling of being isolated with children by inviting friends in.

Mother of two girls aged 1 and 3

" *Everyone knows I'm pretty stuck right now so they've been really good about coming to mine. We had a friend's baby shower here and several birthdays.* "

Travelling

Getting children backwards and forwards between their mother's home and their father's is a major issue in some separated families, and the further apart parents live (and the lower their income) the bigger the problem. Parenting plans sometimes specify the way in which travel should be shared between the parents – often with each being responsible for 50% of the time and money involved – but such arrangements are not always honoured, especially if there are on-going tussles about access.

Travelling by car

If the two homes are only just outside walking or cycling range, driving children between them is usually the quickest and the cheapest method; it may even be the only means of transport since small towns and country areas often have no buses that are even remotely convenient.

Parents who both have cars and are co-operating to make contact visits as comfortable as possible often arrange to do one return journey each.

If the two homes are much further apart, driving may take longer and petrol may cost more than public transport. The car may still score for convenience, though. Some parents share time and expense by each driving half the distance, meeting and transferring the children from one car to the other at an agreed rendezvous.

Public transport

If a child or children can travel alone on public transport from one parent's home to the other, parents save both their time and adult fare-money. Many parents ask how old a child needs to be before such travel is legal and safe.

Buses

- Most bus companies say that a child must be at least eight years old before she can travel alone.
- An eight-year-old who is used to going to school by bus with other children may feel all right about a short, direct journey on her own as long as she is put on by one adult at the beginning and met at the other end. However, if the journey is brief enough to be comfortable for her on her own, it may be little more trouble for one parent to go with her and the other to bring her back. In the course of those accompanied trips she will learn the route and its landmarks so that she becomes more confident about doing the trip alone.

Coaches

- Some coach companies, notably National Express at the time of writing, do not allow children under 14 to travel without someone who is over 16. That is unfortunate because for longer journeys coaches can be much easier than trains for children on their own to manage. Once installed in the right coach the child has no decisions or choices to make; he simply stays put until the coach reaches its terminus where he must be met.

- The requirement that the accompanying person be 16 (rather than a full adult) is helpful to quite a lot of families in which several children, including a 16-year-old, travel to see the other parent.

Trains

- Children have to be eight years old or over before they can travel alone in trains, and some rail companies say that children between eight and 11 can only travel alone in daytime (though it's extremely rare to see that enforced). Whether your child is ready to take a train on her own depends not only on her age, temperament and good sense, but also the line she will be travelling on. Trains that get very full can be daunting and difficult to manage especially as commuting adults seldom treat children as equal human beings.
- If a child needs to get out at an intermediate station rather than the terminus she may have a problem with knowing when she has arrived, Savvy parents provide children with a list of stations the train will stop at and the time it's due at their station. Unfortunately on any day, but most especially Sunday, a child may be faced with unscheduled timetable changes, even a replacement bus service. So 25 minutes on a quiet country route may be fine but a cross-country hour, or a journey that takes her through a big junction such as Reading or Birmingham may not.
- Eurostar has its own regulations that you need to be aware of if your child will be travelling across the English Channel to visit the other parent. The minimum age for travelling alone on Eurostar is 12; furthermore all children between 12 and 16 years need a 'consent to travel' form from you. Journeys by Eurostar are very long for a child.

Planes

- If the non-resident parent moves to a different country, or even to the opposite end of your country, a child's visits may depend on travelling by air. It costs a great deal of money to have an adult actually fly with a child so you will probably want yours to fly alone as soon as possible. When that might be depends not only on the child's age and temperament but also on the kind of journey she has to make.
- An hour-long internal flight from one small airport directly to another may be comparatively easy. You can probably take the child all the way to the plane and all she then has to do is to sit (reasonably) still until she gets off along with everyone else and sees the other parent waiting for her.
- A long international flight is a very different matter because neither you nor the parent meeting her is likely to be allowed

Boy aged 10

" I wanted to go by train 'cause that way I could go to my dad's every weekend not just every other if mum had to drive me. But the first time it got totally packed and a man said I should give up my seat to a grown-up, 'haven't you any manners?' he said, and my bag was under the table and I got pushed away so I thought I wouldn't be able to get it… I did but it wasn't fun. "

past security and she will therefore have to rely on the airline staff employed to look after unaccompanied children. Because of increasing instances of child abduction in custody cases (as well as child trafficking) any immigration officer or airline official may ask you for a letter of 'consent to travel' if your child is crossing national boundaries with one parent alone or with another adult.

- Different airlines have similar but slightly different services and regulations for unaccompanied children. It is important to check the details of the flight you're planning.

- British Airways provides a typical program called the Skyflyer Solo service, which is compulsory for children travelling alone between the ages of five and 12. Children under six can only fly on a single sector non-stop flight. From their sixth birthday they can fly on any BA flight. The same service is available to, but optional for, children between their twelfth and eighteenth birthdays. The service must be booked at the same time as the child's flight ticket. It is expensive. When children fly alone, airlines (like parents!) are most concerned about complications such as transfers and stopovers. BA will not accept a child to travel alone on a journey involving a transfer between London Heathrow and London Gatwick airports. Children are only accepted on journeys that involve a night stop, transfer or stopover exceeding six hours if arrangements have been made for an adult to meet and care for the child at the transfer points. The airline will require full contact details for this person as well as for the person who is to meet the child at the end of the journey.

- If your child is over 12 and eager to travel completely independently, allowing him to do so will save a lot of money. Do bear in mind, though, that if he is making an international flight he will not only have to find his way through security and passport control and to the correct departure gate, he will also have to cope with any travel difficulty that comes up, as if he was an adult passenger. Is he confident enough in talking to adults that he would be able to cope if his baggage was lost, stolen or damaged or his flight was delayed or even diverted to an airport where there will be nobody to meet him? If he is not met, will he manage to communicate with the parent who should be there, and with you? What will you advise him to do? Some airline staff are sympathetic to a child on his own in such circumstances, but your child might get no extra help because staff are too busy with children whose parents have paid for their services, and also, perhaps, too aware that you chose not to.

- If this plane journey is to be an integral part of your child's life for the foreseeable future it's worth doing everything you can to ensure that she doesn't have a nerve-wracking journey early on as if she does she is likely to dread, even resist, doing the same trip later on (see Chapter 8). It will probably be wise – and well worth the expense – to make a trial run with the child before you commit him or her to flying alone. If the child is of primary school-age you might accompany him the first time and use a fly-alone service thereafter. If he is over 12 he may cope easily with a quick internal flight but for a more major trip it might be sensible to use a fly-alone service the first time and let him travel independently the next time, if he still feels confident.

9.3 Boarding schools

For a child whose parents are separating, there may be a period when 'home' is both emotionally and practically chaotic, with short-notice swaps between the care of mother and father or even emergency arrangements for babysitters or people to do the school run. Most parents realise how damaging these levels of unpredictability and insecurity are for their children, but while most will look for ways to bring stability and security back into the home, some, especially the well-to-do, will consider sending the child away from home to find stability in boarding school.

Mother of girl aged 13

> " *I knew we couldn't go on like that. I meant to be home when she got back from school but half the time I was in the middle of yet another agony-discussion with her father and the other half I was in bed with J.*
>
> *I called in every favour I could from school friends' mothers but she hates being foisted on people at no notice. And then there was a weekend when J said 'come to Paris' and I actually got a woman from Universal Aunts to move in. Yes, I'm ashamed. Yes, I wanted her out of the way for my sake but truly it did seem better for her too.* "

Boarding schools have traditionally been seen to provide not only a highly privileged education but also stability and continuity for children whose parents – often in the military, colonial or diplomatic services – had to keep moving so that they would otherwise have had many changes of school. Now that stability and security is increasingly sought by parents such as the mother quoted above. People who are separating worse rather than better and can neither provide, nor allow the other parent to provide, a stable and secure home for their children. Boarding school in term-time and holiday visits to both parents may seem to be the answer, but is it?

Sometimes boarding school can indeed provide a safe place and saving routine for children whose home environments are chaotic. For a looked-after child, for example, a carefully selected boarding school can be a good alternative to yet another foster home. Boarding schools have changed, almost (but not quite) beyond recognition so that some older children, especially teenagers whose focus of attention has begun to move from parents to peers, beg to board. Many schools have day-students as well as boarders and will accommodate children staying full-time, weekly or even on demand, providing all of them with a less institutionalised environment than used to be the case. Day students often say that they miss out on what their school has to offer if they go home each night. However, other children who go to boarding schools – especially younger ones and those who were sent rather than asked to go – are shocked by separation and grieve for home and parents. Even the youngest – tragic six- and seven-year-olds – eventually grow the survival-shell that enables them to pretend they are flourishing: 'I was a bit homesick', they say 'but it was good for me'. They are wrong. It was not.

Woman now aged 60

" *My mother had left my father for another man when I was ten and my father was beyond furious. My mother wanted me to live with her and that's what I wanted too, but although my father didn't want to look after me himself he was determined that she shouldn't. So since she and my stepfather-to-be hadn't married yet he did a sort of moral outrage thing and forbade my mum to have me to stay in their flat. So I was packed off to boarding school. I didn't know what was happening at home. I didn't even really know where home was. I just felt abandoned.* "

If modern boarding schools can be a good experience for some young people, they will not be for those who are sent away from home because separated parents want their own space and privacy or just cannot think what else to do with them. Such children arrive at school as exiles from the family life they knew before. They feel (and are) abandoned and, very often, they feel that the dissolution of life as they knew it is all their fault and this banishment is their punishment. To make matters worse the sentence may seem indefinite because where other homesick children can look forward to returning to their familiar homes and secure families for the next exeat, half-term break or holiday, these children do not know where they will be going or whom they will return to.

- The more muddled the situation is at home, the more important it is that your child should be there so she can see what's happening and, hopefully, see that on some basic level both her parents are 'OK' and still love her.
- If you send her away she will feel (rightly) that she has no control over what is left of her family life or over the decisions being made for her.
- Don't think that by sending your child away you protect her from seeing your unhappiness or the ugly rows that are going on. If she cannot see what is really happening she will imagine much worse.
- Children whose parents are separated are always at risk of feeling that they are somehow responsible: sending your child away will make her feel that she is being banished, and punished.

Boarding schools reduce communication

" [M]issing out on the kind of contact with father we have been discussing is a great loss to a growing child, even if having any father around is becoming a luxury. Moreover, sending children away to boarding school can create a sense of the absence of both mother and father, unless the parents are extremely successful in keeping the emotional channels open with their child. "

Duffell, 2000

9.4 Long-distance parenting

Long-distance parenting is the best that can be managed for one parent in countless numbers of divorced families. We live in a mobile society. It is estimated that in North America the average family changes residences every five years and many families move even more frequently. In intact families relocating can be highly problematic, especially for children, but it is far worse when parents are separated because one parent becomes a long-distance mum or dad and that is one of the most difficult challenges facing divorced parents and their children.

Relocation and the resulting long-distance parenting happens for many different reasons, such as:

- a new or better job or business opportunity
- a transfer or promotion within the current firm (which may or may not be truly optional)
- a new marriage or partnership with someone living in another location
- an employment opportunity for a new partner

- moving close to family for support
- wanting to make a fresh start away from the ex-partner.

A long-term or permanent move to a new country is often harder on children than on their parents, especially when the parents are separated. Whether it is the resident parent who moves abroad, taking the children with her and leaving their father as a long-distance parent, or the other parent who moves abroad leaving his children, those children become long-distance children and the relationship they have with their distant parent, already radically changed by the parents separating, will change again. Sometimes one or more children – often older teenagers – refuse to move with the parent they have always lived with, moving instead to live with the previously non-resident parent.

Long-distance moves inevitably disrupt contact between the children and the non-resident parent. It is not only that many such moves involve enormous distances and therefore demanding and expensive travel for all future contact, but also that despite the ease and ordinariness of tourist travel between countries, crossing borders, even nearby ones, brings separated parents and their parenting plans up against different legal systems and regulations.

Non-resident parents moving further away from children

If you want to move away from where your children live, either within the same country or abroad, you do not require permission or agreement from the resident parent, however much she wants you to stay in close contact with the children, and however certain she feels that your relocation will work against that. Your move may go against the contact arrangements in the parenting plan you made with your ex and even against the advice of advisers, but unlike financial arrangements for maintenance, these are not legal commitments.

Resident parents taking children to live in another country

Helped by globalisation and the boom in relationships between people from different states, an increasing number of separated parents are seeking to emigrate. Relocation to a new country is a positive move for many intact families and may be especially attractive to separated parents seeking a fresh start, but the number of international fights over child custody is going up.

Taking children to live abroad

The number of cases involving parents taking their children to live abroad has risen from 27 in 2007 to a predicted 240 in 2012. Lord Justice Thorpe, head of the office specialising in international family cases, said: 'We acknowledge, as would all individuals concerned or involved with family justice, the additional emotional distress that is caused to any family by the inclusion of an international dimension. It is incumbent upon anyone who works in such a sensitive area to try and find ways of mitigating such stress, to the extent that it is possible to do so.'

Report from the Chief of the Office of the Head of International Family Justice for England and Wales, 2012

Moving abroad with your children

Even if you are the resident parent you cannot make a permanent move abroad with the children without written consent from the other parent. Do be aware of this because if you moved abroad when consent had been refused by your ex, you would have abducted your children, which is, of course, a very serious crime.

- If the contact parent will not agree to your move it will depend on permission from the court.
- If your application to the court is well-prepared, it has a high chance of success though it may be frustratingly slow to be heard. It may be important for you to warn your future employer, landlord or even partner of the length of time that is likely to elapse before you can travel.
- The court will need to be convinced that the move has been meticulously planned, is realistic and would improve the quality of life for the children. The court will want details of your job prospects or family contacts at your destination and will want to be assured that you have immediate accommodation and schooling (if relevant) in place. It will also take account of the wishes of any child who is considered old enough to put her point of view. If all that is in place, the court will tend towards granting your application.
- Some legal professionals believe that permission is sometimes given without due regard to the situation of the other parent and modern thinking on shared parenting. The court will satisfy itself that the proposed move abroad is not an attempt to exclude the other parent from the children's lives, and it will enquire what consideration you have given to the extra

Court decisions on applications to relocate with children

'[D]espite the court's denial that there is any presumption in favour of an applicant for permission to remove, precedents and anecdotal evidence suggest otherwise … In a Resolution debate at the Law Society in September 2005 participants agreed by 77 votes to 19 (with 10 abstentions) that leave to remove is too easily granted … almost all relocation applications are brought by maternal primary carers and almost all of them (and 75% of reported cases) have been granted eventually.'

Gilliatt, 2005

costs of contact after the move, but that is all. The court's consideration of the welfare of the children and whether it is in their best interests to move abroad permanently seldom includes loss of easy access to the other parent.

- The court will, however, try to ensure that contact with the non-resident parent continues, although it will necessarily be more difficult and less frequent. If the court considers that once the move is made contact may not take place it can add conditions, such as a surety or bond payment, to the permission being given. If you then fail to co-operate with contact, the fund could support the travel or even the litigation costs of the contact parent. Realistically, though, unless you plan to relocate to a neighbouring country, the costs of travel will often be prohibitive.
- If your planned new location is many hours flying time away, travel costs are not the only bar to contact; distance and time may also be important. If at least one of the children is very young, good contact between the other parent and that child may have been established and maintained by frequent short visits – days or single overnights – and these will now be impossible (see Chapter 7). Such a long journey will mean that only relatively long visits seem worthwhile, but even two or three such trips each year may take a visiting parent past his leave entitlement and the option of children travelling to visit the parent will only be open to older teenagers and young adults.

Making the best of long-distance parenting

Like almost every situation in post-separation family life, the success of this one for children mostly depends on the relationship between their two parents. If the children live with you and your ex is at a distance, 50% of the responsibility for his continuing relationship with them belongs to you. It's even easier for you to alienate the children from a long-distance parent than from one who is close by and around every weekend, and even more important to be supportive.

- The long-distance parent will have to work at staying in touch with the children using all the methods suggested earlier (see Chapter 7.3). He is far more likely to succeed with your help than without it. For example, you need to help the children manage any time differences and understand when they can and cannot phone or Skype. You need to help your ex set-up a schedule for his calls and make sure the children are there for them.

Long-distance parenting

Fathering from afar may, however, become a skill, which current divorce rates make it imperative for men to learn. I was impressed to see Nelson Mandela talking to Arthur Miller on television, shortly after his release from twenty-seven years in gaol, describing his efforts to father children he had barely known or touched, imparting guidance, boundaries, and love.

Duffell, 2000

- It can be really difficult for a long-distance parent to get information about the children's lives. Share your own and anything you hear from schools, doctors and any sports coaches or out-of-school teachers.
- Look into online programmes (some of them are developed specially for divorced parents) that allow you to provide information about the children that the long-distance parent can access at any time (and vice versa when the children visit him). Parents who have information tend to be more involved and feel more connected to their children.
- Help keep the other parent 'alive' for your child. Don't only allow the children to display formal photos of the long-distance parent, encourage two-way emailing of smartphone photos so they have immediate real-time pictures.
- Do everything you can to make visits possible and enjoyable.

If you are a long-distance parent because your ex has moved away with the children, you may be angry with her and sorry for yourself, but none of that will help the children.

- Remember that as the adult it is up to you to make and maintain contact with the children. Don't sit sadly by, hoping for a phone call or an email. Make one yourself.
- Don't be offended (or worse) if one of the children doesn't call back when you text, or can't wait to get off Skype. These formal communications often interrupt children who are busy with their lives, and then they can't think of anything to say. It helps if you avoid asking questions that have yes/no answers. 'Did you have a good day?' may get you a yes or no and then silence; 'What was the funniest thing that happened today?' might get you a few words and even a giggle. Whichever way it goes try to accept a quick call as the equivalent of a quick hug.
- Set-up a regular schedule for these contacts (especially if you are in separate time zones) and follow it as faithfully as you used to follow the schedule for contact visits. If you say you're going to call, call. If you are going to send an email, do it. Your child needs to be able to count on you following through.

Divorced father of two boys aged 8 and 11

" *When I first heard that she was planning to go and work in Hong Kong I didn't think she really would. Take the boys out of school, out of England, away from me and their grandparents and all their friends? No way… But two weeks later she'd been offered the job; it was clear she was serious and, well, I can honestly say I went into shock. After all the grief and work that went into settling things down after the divorce I was going to lose them. She thought I might refuse my consent and drag the whole thing through the courts but what was the point in making her hate me? It wouldn't have changed anything else in the end.* "

Conclusion

This book started with the importance of looking at family breakdown from the children's points of view, and 200-odd pages later it ends there too. There are many books about divorce – this probably isn't the first you have read – but most of them approach it as adults' business when it is very much children's business as well. I've been aware of this ever since my own family broke-up when I was ten years old, but it's only now, after many years spent researching other aspects of child development and parenting, that turning around the way we handle family breakdown and its impact on children has come to seem both a priority and a possibility. It is a priority because more and more children are being affected, and it is a possibility because recent findings from attachment science show the way.

Right now only about half of all 16 year olds are still living with both their parents, and the number of parents who separate while their children are under five is going up. Research in the last decade is showing us how damaging family breakdown is for children but the way parental separation and divorce is handled is still as adult-centric as ever and our current family law system is still adversarial, still focused on property and profit. Changes are urgently needed. By turning what we now know about the harm parental separation does to children upside down, we can begin to see what can be done to lessen it. Will that happen? Can parents who are separating face up to what that means to their children, and can divorce mediators, solicitors, judges and court advisers focus, and help their clients to focus, on what we now know to be children's essential needs?

Parents matter

The fundamental message of this book is that parents matter even more than we knew and in unexpected ways. That still-growing body of research into brain development offers today's mothers and fathers a new understanding of their own and each other's importance. This is the first generation of parents in a position to realise that from birth, or even before, a child's attachment, first to the mother (or her substitute) and soon also to the father, is responsible not only for his health and happiness today – which is obvious – but also for his entire growth and development as a person, brain and body, now and forever, which is not obvious at all.

Mothers matter most at first

Everything that happens in people's development depends on what happened before, so whatever the age of a child you are concerned for, new knowledge of infancy, the starting point, is vital. Five-sixths of a baby's brain grows after birth and does so astonishingly fast, more than doubling in size in the first year with 40,000 new synapses (connections) forming every second. Only in this generation have we learned that that brain growth is not just a matter of maturation and genetics. The way each individual baby's brain grows and weaves itself together and functions largely depends on his experiences in the last prenatal months and the first year or two after birth.

Significant experiences begin to impinge on that development while a baby is still in his mother's womb, which is why she is uniquely important to him. And even once he is delivered his early experiences continue to centre on his mother, if she is available, or whoever stands in for her if not, so the emotional relationship he shares and builds with her is the foundation of all that is to follow: the actual structure and functioning of his brain, his personality, the way he will manage his feelings and relationships and cope with stress throughout his life.

At birth, the left hand 'thinking' part of a baby's brain is yet to develop. His right-brain (and newly-separated body) experiences and reacts to deep, primitive feelings: to fear and anger, to excitement and joy, but because he himself does not have the brain capacity to regulate those potentially overwhelming feelings he relies on his primary attachment figure to lend him the use of her brain to keep his feelings in balance and bring him back from terror or excitement to calm.

A baby's primary attachment figure can, of course, be his father, but it will usually be his mother, not only because her relationship with the baby got a head start while he was inside her but also because most (though not all) females are better than most (but not all) males at right-brain responsiveness. A mother who is attuned to her baby responds to his right-brain with her own. When he cries, she does not need to use her adult, developed left-brain to think about what she has heard or plan what she will do about it; she simply responds, often leaving the TV and starting up the stairs before she is conscious of having heard that cry. She and her baby communicate without words or conscious thought, using facial expressions, different emotionally-loaded tones of voice (including motherese) and a lot of touching, gesturing and hugging.

All this baby-stuff that used to be taken as much for granted as petting a puppy, and even rationed for fear of 'spoiling', is now known to be enormously important to a child's development. A baby's right-brain cannot grow and develop fully without these intimate human experiences. They are what get imprinted into his brain's circuits. And how a mother provides those experiences for him largely depends on the emotional experiences that were imprinted and stored in the circuits of *her* right-brain when she was an infant with *her* mother. These nonverbal communication skills that we learn in infancy are used throughout our lives in all our interpersonal and intimate relationships, including romantic or marital partnerships. And their patterns tend to repeat across generations. Family breakdown often contributes to disturbed childhood attachment, but childhood attachment stressors also play a big part in divorce and the custody battles that so often follow.

Fathers soon matter just as much

It is because a baby's primary attachment starts in the womb and is almost always to his mother that accounts of infant development tend to imply that mothers are the primary parents and fathers secondary. That is a misreading of the facts. A child's relationships with each parent are equally important but different both in timing and in kind. In the right-brain-dominated first year what babies need most is maternal regulation of otherwise uncontrollable emotions: soothing and reassurance. But as long as the father is sufficiently available the baby will be gradually building an attachment to him that will intensify in the second year, when the left-brain enters a growth spurt. Now, exploration and understanding of the physical world come to the fore, supported by new experiences and challenges provided by father's attention and play.

People go on developing attachments all through their lives – to other family members, to adults from outside the family such as teachers, to childhood and adolescent 'best friends' and eventually to adult sexual partners – but these first attachments are the foundation of all that follow.

Parental separation is worse for the children

Fresh understanding of the full extent of both parents' importance to their children throws the significance of family breakdown into sharp relief. Parental separation or divorce is very seldom pain-free for anyone, but it is clear now that because relationships with parents are central to children's lifelong development it is most damaging to them. Furthermore, no child is too young or too old to be affected by it. Whether the offspring of separating parents is six months or six, 16 or 26 years old, having the family split-up and mother and father living separately from each other and interacting with her only one at a time will always be emotionally as well as practically disruptive, miserable, bewildering and sad.

Parents sometimes assume that babies who are too young to understand what is going on are too young to be damaged by it, but a baby's relationship with that 'primary carer' (usually, though not always, mum) is the most important aspect of his world and anything that upsets or distracts her will impinge on him, even before he is born. At the other end of childhood, parents are not entitled to congratulate themselves on delaying a long-planned separation until the children are old enough to 'understand'. What those adult children are likely to take from their parents' long-delayed separation is that their personal history was built on lies and that their childhood memories and sense of identity are false.

These are not messages parents, grandparents or step-parents-in-the-making want to hear, so people don't talk much about the effects on children of parents separating. Considering that about half of all children live through and with family breakdown it is astonishing how little it is acknowledged. If half the children in your child's school year faced a physical disaster, such as losing a limb, everyone would be talking about it all the time. As it is, though, when discussion does take place it usually stresses how resilient children are and how quickly they'll get over it. Unfortunately, that's wishful thinking. Children are not born resilient (though they will become more so if their attachments in the first years are secure) and their parents' parting is too basic a fracture in their social and emotional development for them to 'get over it' in the sense of putting it behind them and getting on with life as it would have been. Children adapt to new circumstances and relationships – what choice do they have? – but even when they seem to have healed there will be scars remaining.

Despite the efforts of some individuals, the current adversarial family law system does nothing to help separating parents protect their children. The way family courts deal with separation and custody sometimes even encourages parents to fight and to make outrageous claims about each other's behaviour instead of encouraging reconciliation and ensuring that children's needs are met in practice as well as in theory. And although most parents at first intend to protect their children from adult fall-out many become so submerged in their own disrupted lives, anger and hurt that they may unwittingly unleash in their offspring a lifetime of upset, misplaced guilt and conflicted loyalty.

It should be understood that these pages do not aim to suggest that because family breakdown is so bad parents should stay together 'for the sake of the children'. An unhappy partnership held together only by duty is unlikely to last for long in our current 'me culture', where personal fulfilment is almost a duty, and is unlikely to make for good parenting or happy children in the meantime. Vague long-term dissatisfaction isn't as obvious as open parental irritation or depression, or the sexual unfaithfulness, arguments, enmity and especially violence that poison many children's growing-up, but if the long-term relationship between parents has become joyless or intolerable to one or both of them it will be a chilly environment for their children today and model loveless relationships for them as they grow up.

Putting children first

We have to accept separation and divorce as a counterbalance to failed cohabitation and marriage. Contemporary society, where many people live into their eighties, cannot manage without it. But the wellbeing of the children who will grow up to form that society in their turn is being put at unnecessary risk by the way that safety valve is deployed. It is clear that it could be managed better. Instead of asking 'should people stay together for the children's sake?' we should be asking 'can women and men who cannot live in peaceful comfort together be better mothers and fathers when they are apart?' The question is rarely asked, because who gets divorced in order to be a better parent? And if it was asked the answer would be assumed to be 'no'. But it is clear that when separating adults can make the needs of the children their priority the answer is often 'yes'.

Everyone pays lip-service to the notion of putting children first but actually doing it is not something everybody takes for granted. This is a 'me society' and some parents ask why children's happiness should come first: is their own happiness not just as important? The simple answer is that people-who-are-parents may divorce or leave each other but cannot divorce and should not ever leave their children, not only because children's current happiness and wellbeing depends on them but also because children's development into the adults of the future is at stake. If we want to be really me-me-me about it we should think about how those children will care for us when *we're* dependent on *them*.

Making the best of a bad job

There's no escaping the fact that family breakdown is always a bad break for everyone, but the message of this book is not all doom and gloom. If we are aware of, understand and learn from the same growing body of research that shows how damaging separation can be, we can make the best of that bad job for children.

A vital first step is to reverse the adult-centric way parental separation is dealt with, not only in families but often in lawyers' offices and family courts too. When a family breaks down everyone's energy goes into fighting for or trying to reconcile the interests of father and mother. An important and often-ignored fact coming out of that research is that children's interests may be entirely different.

Treating children as people rather than possessions

Parental separation means a lot of sharing out, and in the name of 'equal parenting' children are too often shared between parents like the DVD collection or the savings. But children are not chattels. Contact or custody arrangements that seem 'fair' to the parent or the court may be not just 'unfair' but damagingly wrong for a child. In the long-term fathers are as important as mothers, and many studies now show that children, adolescents and adults who have close relationships with their fathers do better everywhere and forever – at school, at work and in their social lives – than those who do not, so it is clearly highly desirable that children of all ages should have the best possible relationship with both parents. But what about the short-term? When a lawyer bids for his client to have his baby son to live with him at weekends they are both ignoring clear evidence that overnight separations from the mother are not only usually distressing but also potentially damaging to the brain development and secure attachment of any child under about four. And when people say that it is 'only fair' for a father and mother to care for their five-year-old daughter on alternate weeks, they mean that it is fair to the adults irrespective of what it means to the child. These arrangements sometimes seem to be made by people who are seeing a child as a possession and her presence as their right, rather than seeing her as a person who needs both parents but also needs to live somewhere she can call home.

Mutual parenting

So the final lessons these same research data can teach go full circle, to our new understanding of the overwhelming importance to children of their relationships with parents. They tell us that when a marriage or partnership has definitely ended what matters most to children of any age is that parenting has not. When relationships between wives and husbands fail, children's relationships with mothers and fathers must at all costs be protected and maintained. Those costs can be high (outside as well as inside a lawyer's office) because, as the many children's voices in this book make clear, the needs and wants of a particular child may be completely different from the needs and wants of her father or her mother and it is the child, with her whole future development as a person ahead of her, who must come first.

It is difficult for anyone who has not been in that position to imagine what it costs a loving father to acknowledge that if he and his partner cannot live together, living with the mother is probably better for their baby than living with him. And it is equally difficult to imagine the cost to a mother who, while bruised by betrayal and furious with her ex, must nevertheless acknowledge and act on the fact that the children still love and need their daddy.

When a family breaks down what matters most to children of all ages is not their parents' physical separation but their enmity. The separated parents who do their children most damage are those who fight over them and try to alienate them from the other parent; such parenting is broken. Children survive family breakdown better if parents can confine their adult issues, anger and bitterness to their woman–man relationship, so that their relationship as mother–father can remain polite. But what will best ease the children through their inevitable misery when the family unit is broken is for separated partners to muster selfless concern for the children. That selfless concern can keep them united in their determination to carry on being, and helping each other to be, loving parents. I have called that mutual parenting, and it is the best possible way forward from family breakdown. No longer a wife, husband or partner, but always and forever a mother or father.

References

American Psychological Association (2013) *The Changing Role of the Modern Day Father*. Available at: http://apa.org/pi/families/resources/changing-father.aspx.

Brown, A. and Jones, J. M. (2012) *Separation, Divorce Linking to Sharply Lower Wellbeing*. Available at: http://www.gallup.com/poll/154001/separation-divorce-linked-sharply-lower-wellbeing.aspx.

Casey, B.J., Jones, R.M. and Hare, T.A. (2008) 'The adolescent brain', *Annals of the New York Academy of Sciences* 1124: pp.111–26.

Cheadle, J.E., Amato, P.R. and King, V. (2010) 'Patterns of nonresidential father contact', *Demography* 47(1): pp.205–25.

Crittenden, P.M. and Claussen, A.H. (2000) *The Organization of Attachment Relationships: Maturation, Culture, and Context*, New York: Cambridge University Press, pp.343–57.

Deblaquiere, J., Moloney, L. and Weston, R. (2012) 'Parental separation and grandchildren: the multiple perspectives of grandparents', *Family Matters* 90: pp.68–76.

Duffell, N. (2000) *The Making of Them: The British Attitude to Children and the Boarding School System*, London: Lone Arrow Press.

The Gallup Organisation. 'Separation, Divorce Linked to Sharply Lower Wellbeing'. 2014 [Online] Available at: http://www.gallup.com/poll/154001/separation-divorce-linked-sharply-lower-wellbeing.aspx.

Gilliatt, J. (2005) 'I'm leaving on a jet plane, don't know when I'll be back again: can I take the kids with me?', *Family Law* Journal. Available at: www.familylawweek.co.uk.

Gingerbread (n.d.) Statistics. Available at: http://www.gingerbread.org.uk/content/365/Statistics.

Judiciary of England and Wales (2012) A*nnual Report* [Online]. Available at: https://www.judiciary.gov.uk/Resources/JCO/Documents/Reports/international_family_justice_2013.pdf.

The King's Fund (2012) *British Social Attitudes survey 2012: public satisfaction with the NHS and its services*. Available at: http://www.kingsfund.org.uk/projects/bsa-survey-2012.

Kirkland Weir, I. (2009) *When did you last see your father?* [talk to Hertfordshire Family Forum]. 26 November. Available at: http://www.neves-solicitors.co.uk/site/library/privategeneral/WhenDidYouLastSeeYourFather.html

Lagattuta, K.H., Sayfan, L. and Bamford, C. (2012) 'Do you know how I feel? Parents underestimate worry and overestimate optimism compared to child self-report', *J Exp Child Psychol* 113(2): pp.211–32.

Leach, P. (1994) *Children First*, New York: Vintage, pp.9, 146–68.

Leach, P. (2010a) *Your Baby and Child*, London: Dorling Kindersley, p.523.

Leach, P. (2010b) *Childcare Today*, New York: Vintage, pp.115–24.

Lewis, C. and Lamb, M.E. (2007) *Understanding Fatherhood: A Review of Recent Research*, London: Joseph Rowntree Foundation.

McIntosh, J.E. (2011) 'Special considerations for infants and toddlers in separation/divorce'. Available at: www.child-encyclopedia.com/documents/McIntoshANGxp1.pdf, pp.1–6.

Metsa-Simola, N. and Martikainen, P. (2013a) 'Divorce and changes in the prevalence of psychotropic medication use: a register-based longitudinal study among middle-aged Finns', *Soc Sci Med* 94: pp.71–80.

Metsa-Simola, N. and Martikainen, P. (2013b) 'The short-term and long-term effects of divorce on mortality risk in a large Finnish cohort, 1990–2003', *Popul Stud (Camb)* 67(1): pp.97–110.

Millward, C. (1998) *Family Relationship and Intergenerational Exchange in Later Life*, working paper No. 15, Melbourne: Australian Institute of Family Studies.

Mindful Policy Group (2014) *The Pledge for Children*. Available at: http://www.mindfulpolicygroup.com/policy-areas/the-pledge-for-children/.

Nielsen, L., Fabricius, W.V., Kruk, E. and Emery, R.E. (2012) 'Shared parenting: facts & fiction', *Timeless Attachments: Research and Policy Implications*, Chicago, IL, 2012, Workshop 26, AFCC 49th Annual Conference.

Office for National Statistics (2014) *Marriages, Cohabitations, Civil Partnerships and Divorces*. Available at: http://www.ons.gov.uk/ons/taxonomy/index.html?nscl=Marriages,+Cohabitations,+Civil+Partnerships+and+Divorces.

Rodda, M., Hallgarten, J. and Freeman, J. (2013) *Between the cracks: exploring in-year admissions in schools in England*. Available at: http://www.thersa.org/__data/assets/pdf_file/0007/1527316/RSA_Education_Between_the_cracks_report.pdf.

Schore, A.N. and McIntosh, J. (2011) 'Attachment theory and the emotional revolution in neuroscience', *Family Court Review* 49(3): 501–512.

Sexton, R., McIntosh, J. and Hon. Dickler, G.G. (2012) 'Parenting arrangements for the 0–4 year group', *Infants, attachment and the courtroom: practical guidelines for the busy judge*, AFCC 49th Annual Conference. Chicago, IL, 2012, Workshop 32.

Thompson, H. (2011) *Home Alone*. Available at: http://yougov.co.uk/news/2011/02/17/home-alone/.

United Nations Economic Commission for Europe (2014) *Statistics*. Available at: http://www.unece.org/stats/stats_h.html.

Warnes, T. and Crane, M. (2004) *Homelessness in the over-fifties*, Report by the Economic and Social Research Council.

Index

Subscribers

Unbound is a new kind of publishing house. Our books are funded directly by readers. This was a very popular idea during the late eighteenth and early nineteenth centuries. Now we have revived it for the internet age. It allows authors to write the books they really want to write and readers to support the writing they would most like to see published.

The names listed below are of readers who have pledged their support and made this book happen. If you'd like to join them, visit: www.unbound.co.uk.

Jane McDonagh, Partner, Family Law,
at Simons Muirhead & Burton.
T: +44 (0) 203 206 2700
Jane.McDonagh@smab.co.uk
Simons Muirhead & Burton, 8–9 Frith Street,
London, W1D 3JB

Jonathan Akass, Media Citizens
T: +44 (0) 207 378 1448
info@mediacitizens.com
Media Citizens, 2 Sudley Street, London, SE1 1PF

Tim Langton, Senior Partner at Goodman Derrick LLP
T: +44 (0) 207 404 0606
TLangton@gdlaw.co.uk
Goodman Derrick LLP, 10 St Bride Street,
London, EC4A 4AD

Victoria Scott, Victoria Scott Mediation
T: +44 (0) 795 846 6042
enquiries@victoriascottmediation.com
Victoria Scott Mediation, Muswell Hill, North London

Charlotte Bradley, Kingsley Napley LLP

Hetty Gleave, Hunters Solicitors

Jane Auld, The National Parenting Initiative

Sean McNally, Ellis Jones

Wilsons Solicitors

Flo Atkins

Dr. Christine Bidmead

Dan Brooke

Maureen Buchanan

Xander Cansell

Georgina Cole

Geoffrey Darnton

Angela de Mille

Diana Dean

DJL

Gien Donovan

Christopher Dudman

Katherine Edward

Susan Evans

Maria Foldvari

Dominic Frisby

Sue Gerhardt

Rosy Glover

Judith Golberg

Freja Gregory

Ann Horne

Nancy Ireland

Yvonne Johnson

David Keighley

Hilary Kennedy

Dan Kieran

Sebastian Kraemer

Miriam Landor

Jimmy Leach

Melissa Leach

Tim Loughton

Meryl McCartney

Colin Maginn

The Ministry of Parenting

David Morton

Susan Park

C Miranda Passey

Don Peterkin

Richard Phillips

Rebeca Robertson

Mary Robson

Andrew Rosenfeld

Christoph Sander

Dr. David A. Seager

Polly Shand

Sheila Simpson

Peter Smith

Juliet Soskice

Kate Springford

Janine Sternberg

Peter Thickett

Susan Trussell

Laura Vicars

Zoe Wilson

A note about the typefaces

The typeface used in this book is Glypha LT Std. Designed by the Swiss typographer Adrian Frutiger in 1977 for Monotype Imaging, Glypha is based on his earlier, enormously successful Univers typeface.

Frutiger, one of the leading lights in the creation of digital typography during the latter portion of the century, designed Univers in 1954, when he was only 28. He was inspired to create a sans serif typeface by the example of the Berthold Type Foundry's Akzidenz Grotesk, which was created in 1896. The realist, neo-grotesque model that resulted bears strong similarities to two other typefaces also based on Akzidenz Grotesk: Folio and Neue Haas Grotesk (later renamed Helvetica). Though the three were all released in the same year, Univers remains distinct due to the unique weighting of its numbers.

Univers became standard for Paris Metro signage in the 1970s and soon after became common in signage around the world. Glypha, while less-known than Univers, is nonetheless highly distinctive for a slab serif in that the stroke weights vary slightly.